"There may not be any greater need in this moment—for both the church and the larger culture—than a practical theology of the news. *Reading the Times* is a book that addresses a discipleship crisis of our day. It may be a generation too late, but it's not a moment too soon."

Karen Swallow Prior, author of *On Reading Well: Finding the Good Life Through Great Books*

"I am so grateful for a book that steps back from the flash and distraction of headlines to think deeply about the purpose of the news and how Christians are called to engage. In *Reading the Times*, Jeffrey Bilbro provides readers with a theological framework for our contemporary discourse. He offers examples from the tradition, from the Old Testament to modern heroes of the faith, such as Frederick Douglass and Dorothy Day, that we might apprentice ourselves, as Bilbro puts it, before these models. Like a teacher, Bilbro questions readers about our ways of responding to media, and he leads us to consider how our participation with contemporary news forms us and our community. By contextualizing our reading of the news within kairos, Bilbro shows Christians how, as T. S. Eliot writes, 'to apprehend the point of intersection of the timeless with time.' A relevant and timeless book about how Christians should belong in but not of this world."

Jessica Hooten Wilson, Louise Cowan Scholar in Residence at the University of Dallas, author of *Giving the Devil His Due: Flannery O'Connor and The Brothers Karamazov*

"Jeffrey Bilbro's *Reading the Times* makes a compelling sweep of material, technological, and philosophical history, helping Christians ask pressing contemporary questions: How do we attend faithfully to the news? To what political, moral, social, and spiritual ends do we scroll Twitter, check Facebook, and scan the morning headlines? Attention deficit, hyperpartisanship, and misinformation are familiar problems in our current media landscape, but Bilbro goes beyond these standard diagnoses. In the Augustinian tradition, he examines not just media consumption but media appetite. I find his work both practical and prophetic: one foot in chronos, one in kairos, Bilbro begs us to fight for better media habits and rightly ordered media loves. I hope people will gather together around these pages and attend to them slowly, prayerfully, resolutely."

Jen Pollock Michel, author of *A Habit Called Faith* and *Surprised by Paradox*

"*Reading the Times* is essential reading for today's Christian. Jeffrey Bilbro helps us recognize the philosophical and epistemological narratives underlying current headlines and debates, and he gives his readers a deeper understanding of the life we're cultivating for ourselves when we pick up our newspapers or scroll through our news feeds. Centered on the gospel and its timeless beauty, this book proffers a far better vision for our news consumption and public witness, showing us how we can begin to cultivate sound minds and lives of grace."

Gracy Olmstead, journalist and author of *Uprooted: Recovering the Legacy of the Places We've Left Behind*

Reading
the
Times

A Literary and Theological
Inquiry into the News

Jeffrey Bilbro

Academic

An imprint of InterVarsity Press
Downers Grove, Illinois

InterVarsity Press
P.O. Box 1400, Downers Grove, IL 60515-1426
ivpress.com
email@ivpress.com

InterVarsity Press® is the book-publishing division of InterVarsity Christian Fellowship/USA®, a movement of students and faculty active on campus at hundreds of universities, colleges, and schools of nursing in the United States of America, and a member movement of the International Fellowship of Evangelical Students. For information about local and regional activities, visit intervarsity.org.

Scripture quotations, unless otherwise noted, are from The Holy Bible, English Standard Version, copyright © 2001 by Crossway Bibles, a division of Good News Publishers. Used by permission. All rights reserved.

While any stories in this book are true, some names and identifying information may have been changed to protect the privacy of individuals.

Figure 1.1. The First American Macadam Road, 1823, by Carl Rakeman, used courtesy of Federal Highway Administration, United States Department of Transportation.

Figure 2.1. Solitude, 1933, by Marc Chagall, © 2020 Artists Rights Society (ARS), New York / ADAGP, Paris, used by permission.

Figure 6.1. Luke Anthology, Donald Jackson with contributions from Aidan Hart and Sally Mae Joseph, © 2002, The Saint John's Bible, Saint John's University, Collegeville, Minnesota USA. Used by permission. All rights reserved.

Figure 8.1. The Liberator, 1861, art by Hammatt Billings, engraving by Alonzo Hartwell, from Boston Public Library, Rare Books Department, Anti-Slavery Collection Digital Commonwealth: www.digitalcommonwealth.org/search/commonwealth:mc87rc937, public domain.

Cover design and image composite: David Fassett
Interior design: Daniel van Loon
Image: © David Crunelle / EyeEm / Getty Images

ISBN 978-0-8308-4185-1 (print)
ISBN 978-0-8308-4186-8 (digital)

Printed in the United States of America ♾

InterVarsity Press is committed to ecological stewardship and to the conservation of natural resources in all our operations. This book was printed using sustainably sourced paper.

Library of Congress Cataloging-in-Publication Data
A catalog record for this book is available from the Library of Congress.

| **P** | 22 | 21 | 20 | 19 | 18 | 17 | 16 | 15 | 14 | 13 | 12 | 11 | 10 | 9 | 8 | 7 | 6 | 5 | 4 | 3 | 2 | 1 |
| **Y** | 39 | 38 | 37 | 36 | 35 | 34 | 33 | 32 | 31 | 30 | 29 | 28 | 27 | 26 | 25 | 24 | 23 | 22 | 21 |

To Melissa and Hannah,

with whom I am grateful to be on pilgrimage.

Hannah's oft-repeated "Look at me, Daddy!" reminds me

to attend to what is most newsworthy in my life.

But to apprehend
The point of intersection of the timeless
With time, is an occupation for the saint—
No occupation either, but something given
And taken, in a lifetime's death in love,
Ardour and selflessness and self-surrender.

. . . .

These are only hints and guesses,
Hints followed by guesses; and the rest
Is prayer, observance, discipline, thought and action.
The hint half guessed, the gift half understood, is Incarnation.

T. S. ELIOT, "DRY SALVAGES"

Contents

Acknowledgments

ALTHOUGH I'M RATHER CRITICAL of social media in this book, I should begin by confessing that this project was sparked by a Twitter conversation. Noah Toly and Martyn Wendell Jones exchanged tweets about the need for a book on how Christians should consume the news. That was the provocation I needed to begin organizing some long-standing thoughts and ideas I had on this topic. When I tweeted that I was drafting a book in response, Jon Boyd wrote me to express his interest in the project. So my thanks go to Noah and Martyn (and even, I suppose, to Twitter, or really to the wonderful people who find ways to use that tool redemptively); I'm sure this isn't the book they had in mind, but I hope it proves to be helpful to some readers nonetheless.

Writing can be a lonely endeavor, but I'm grateful for my family, friends, and colleagues who discussed some of these ideas with me, read drafts, and reminded me that belonging well precedes thinking well. My parents read and commented on a full draft, and many of my colleagues at Spring Arbor University asked me hard questions that made the final version better. Jon's keen editorial eye and the comments from IVP's anonymous readers also guided my revisions. If stupid claims remain, I have only myself to blame. I'm also grateful for the course release that Spring Arbor University granted me to complete this book and for the remarkable team of librarians at the White Library.

The *Front Porch Republic* community has been a source of great encouragement to me: Matt Stewart and Eric Miller in particular helped me hone some of my thinking on these matters. When I told Jason Peters I was working on a book about how we should read the news, he replied, "That would be a short book if I wrote it: 'Ignore it.'" Despite his judgment of the subject, he has been much kinder to the author.

The dedication records my greatest debt.

Introduction

Reading the News in Order to Love Our Neighbors

IN EARLY 2017, less than a month after Donald Trump was inaugurated as the president of the United States, the *Washington Post* adopted a new slogan: "Democracy Dies in Darkness."[1] There is of course a long tradition that sees a free and independent press as essential to a healthy democracy and the common good. In our postfact culture, moreover, paeans to the importance of the press have grown increasingly emphatic. And for good reason: the media can host a thoughtful, informed conversation around the issues of our day, and such a conversation does indeed serve the common good. Yet, when we are inundated with stories and issues that demand our attention, it seems rather naive to think that democracy will be preserved if we simply have more news, more fact checking, more investigative reporting, and more deep dives. We don't just need the media to cast a more piercing light; rather, as consumers of the news, we need to reevaluate the light we rely on to understand our times and discern how to respond.

In the prologue to his Gospel, John directs our attention to a different light: the Word who is "the light [that] shines in the

[1]Paul Farhi, "The Washington Post's New Slogan Turns Out to Be an Old Saying," *Washington Post*, February 24, 2017, www.washingtonpost.com/lifestyle/style/the-washington-posts-new-slogan-turns-out-to-be-an-old-saying/2017/02/23/cb199cda-fa02-11e6-be05-1a3817ac21a5_story.html.

darkness." And John reassures us that "the darkness has not overcome it" (Jn 1:5). John urges us to place our faith not in the light shed by the news of the moment but in the light of the good news that speaks time itself into existence. The primary light we need to participate in democracy, to serve the common good, and to dwell as faithful citizens of the City of God is shed not by the *Washington Post* but by "the light of the world" (Jn 8:12). How might we begin living by this light now, in the midst of a world where darkness often seems to prevail?

For centuries Christians, particularly in the Protestant tradition, saw printing technologies and the freedom of the press as handmaidens to the light of the gospel. Yet matters seem more fraught in our digital-media ecosystem. Ivan Illich's understanding of technological change may illuminate this historical trajectory. Illich claims that when industrial technologies replace traditional tools, there is an initial inflection point at which industrialization introduces significant improvements. However, at some later point, the industrialized tools begin causing new problems and "the marginal utility of further" professionalization and industrialization declines. After this second watershed is passed, the application of industrial technologies causes more harm than good. In the context of medicine, Illich locates the first watershed around 1913 as germ theory and new medicines led to marked improvement in people's health. But by the 1950s, iatrogenic diseases—those induced by the medical system—were on the rise, and "the cost of healing was dwarfed by the cost of extending sick life." Illich traces a similar trajectory in many spheres of life, including "education, the mails, social work, transportation, and even civil engineering."[2] If, in the context of media technologies, Gutenberg's press represents

---

[2]Ivan Illich, *Tools for Conviviality* (London: Marion Boyars, 2001), 6-7.

the first watershed, the second watershed may have been the application of steam power to printing. Digital media have recapitulated this cycle: if the first watershed of digital texts was crossed at some point in the early 1990s, the second one may be marked by the 2007 release of the iPhone. As smartphones became ubiquitous, a few companies—Facebook, Google, and Amazon in particular—consolidated and monetized the more decentralized flow of information that marked the early days of the internet.

In this digitized media ecosystem, the light of the news media may distract from the light of the gospel as often as it serves it. While the *Washington Post* claims that democracy dies in darkness, democracy can also die in hypermedia's garish light. The celebrity gossip, ephemeral political drama, and quirky distractions that dominate our media don't serve the common good. Keeping up to date with the latest funny video or outrageous statement that pulses through our social media feeds doesn't bolster democracy. The top story on *BuzzFeed News* this morning exemplifies this genre: "This Woman Pretended to Be a Bush During Her Sister's Engagement and It's Pretty Funny."[3] And this is a relatively innocuous example. Media critics like Daniel Boorstin, Neil Postman, and John Sommerville have argued that the news media *create* these pseudoevents that make up so much of the drama that fills television broadcasts and newspaper pages.[4]

---

[3]Lauren Strapagiel, "This Woman Pretended to Be a Bush During Her Sister's Engagement and It's Pretty Funny," *BuzzFeed News*, September 30, 2019, www.buzzfeednews.com/article/laurenstrapagiel/sister-bush-proposal-ghillie -surprise.

[4]Daniel J. Boorstin, *The Image: A Guide to Pseudo-Events in America* (New York: Vintage, 1992); Neil Postman, *Amusing Ourselves to Death: Public Discourse in the Age of Show Business* (New York: Penguin, 1986); and C. John Sommerville, *How the News Makes Us Dumb: The Death of Wisdom in an Information Society* (Downers Grove, IL: InterVarsity Press, 2009).

Many of the "events" that compose the news emerging from Washington, DC, or New York City or Hollywood are Baudrillardian simulacra, representations designed to amuse and distract but whose relation to reality is tangential at best.[5] Even when serious events are happening—when a pandemic is sweeping the world, or police are killing African Americans, or Congress is deliberating the passage of momentous laws—they can be trivialized through memes and hashtags and co-opted by simplistic partisan narratives.

Indeed, one reason it is so difficult to discern how to follow the news is that our news media have become incredibly diverse. They include TV and radio broadcasts as well as thirty-second video clips and podcasts, newspapers and magazines as well as blogs, and long-form journalism as well as tweets and Facebook posts. All these forms are interdependent: serious essays are now written in response to Twitter spats. Moreover, links to cat videos, political advertisements, thoughtful essays, conspiracy theories, your cousin's wedding announcement, political commentary, and an *Atlantic* cover story sit alongside one another in your social media feed. It is difficult to know how to navigate this chaotic landscape prudently, and of course it's even more of a challenge for the journalists who are striving to discern the lineaments of God's kingdom in the events of today and to consider how we might be called to participate in his ongoing work. Many contemporary journalists would attest to the challenges that our media ecosystem and its perverse incentives pose to producing good, redemptive stories.

I'll endeavor to differentiate among some of these varieties of media, but it's also important to recognize the ways they are intertwined. Further, our posture toward these media often

---

[5]Jean Baudrillard, *Simulacra and Simulation*, trans. Sheil Faria Glaser (Ann Arbor: University of Michigan Press, 1994).

reveals underlying moral and social failures: our failure to attend to what and whom we ought, our failure to recognize what actions are appropriate to our moment, and our failure to belong well to one another. A topic as seemingly discrete as "the news" ends up having far-reaching implications.

These profound implications mean that we cannot ignore current events simply because much that passes for news today is trivial or vapid. Nor do journalists deserve the browbeating to which they are too often subjected. Instead, we would do well to apprentice ourselves to a long tradition—stretching from the Old Testament prophets to Jesus to the church fathers to many saintly contemplatives and social advocates—that models a way of responding wisely to contemporary events. In the pages that follow, I'll point to figures such as Henry David Thoreau, Blaise Pascal, Simone Weil, Thomas Merton, Dante, Frederick Douglass, and Dorothy Day as exemplars in this tradition. Their insights can teach us to be grateful for the good work of secular journalists who shed light on injustice—people like Art Cullen, a writer for *The Storm Lake Times* in rural Iowa who won the Pulitzer Prize in 2017 for his editorials "that successfully challenged powerful corporate agricultural interests in Iowa."[6] And they also teach us to value Christian journalists and news organizations who strive to understand the affairs of our day by the light of the eternal Word. *World Magazine*'s annual Hope Awards, for instance, highlight several nonprofits each year with the goal of honoring "a few of the self-sacrificing Christian helpers in neighborhoods throughout the United States and [profiling] groups that have built replicable programs."[7]

---

[6]Pulitzer Prizes, "Art Cullen of *The Storm Lake Times*, Storm Lake, IA," 2017, www.pulitzer.org/winners/art-cullen.

[7]"Directory of Hope Awards Finalists," *World*, accessed July 20, 2020, https://world.wng.org/content/directory_of_hope_awards_finalists.

Framing the importance of the news in terms of democracy may not offer sufficient guidance, although it's a fine place to start. But, as Christians, we should seek to attend to contemporary affairs as citizens of heaven who have been called to love our neighbors here and now. What do we need to know to love our neighbors well? Or, to frame the question differently, to what do we need to attend in order to live faithfully in this place and in this time? These are the questions the gospel calls us to answer, and they are much more compelling and difficult questions than asking simply what we need to know to be informed voters.

To answer these questions, we need a practical theology of the news. While others have written perceptively regarding how Christian theology might guide news *producers*—Marvin Olasky's *Reforming Journalism* comes to mind—my aim is to think theologically about how Christians should *consume* the news.[8] In the pages that follow I consider how a Christian account of attention, time, and community might inform our relation to the news. Each of the book's three parts addresses a more particular question: To what should we attend? How should we imagine and experience time? How should we belong to one another? In responding to these questions, each part follows a similar arc: the initial chapter considers how our contemporary media ecosystem offers inadequate answers to these questions, the second chapter proposes a theological answer (and includes examples of Christians who embodied this answer), and the final chapter identifies specific practices by which we might cultivate a healthier posture toward the news. Reading the news well requires a good, theological understanding of the news, but that theology also needs to be

---

[8]Marvin Olasky, *Reforming Journalism* (Phillipsburg, NJ: P&R, 2019).

instantiated in healthy habits. For, as authors such as Tish Harrison Warren and Justin Earley have recently argued, regardless of what we say we believe, it's our daily habits that reveal and shape our actual theology.[9]

We are living through a time when technological, economic, and political forces are causing drastic upheavals in the news industry. These changes are provoking an outpouring of essays and books about how to save journalism and what the news industry should look like in a digital age. But I want to take a step back and gain some theological and historical perspective on the more fundamental questions about the very purpose of news. If we have a better understanding of what the news is for—and what it's not for—we will be better able to produce wise reports and analyses of contemporary events and to respond to these charitably. When the news sets itself up as the light of the world, it is usurping the role that rightly belongs only to the Word proclaimed in the gospel. But when the news helps us attend together to the ongoing work of this Word, it plays a vital role in enabling us to love our neighbors.

---

[9]Tish Harrison Warren, *Liturgy of the Ordinary: Sacred Practices in Everyday Life* (Downers Grove, IL: InterVarsity Press, 2016); and Justin Whitmel Earley, *The Common Rule: Habits of Purpose for an Age of Distraction* (Downers Grove, IL: InterVarsity Press, 2019).

PART 1

Attention

Chapter One

Macadamized Mind

WE MAY THINK that the digital era introduces fundamentally new dynamics to the media ecosystem. In many ways, however, digital technologies have simply amplified the dynamics created by the industrial revolution: it was steam power, not binary code, that birthed the modern news industry. One of the most prescient prophets who warned about the effects of this dangerous abundance of news and entertainment was Henry David Thoreau. The popular caricature of Thoreau as a hermit fails to recognize his deep commitment to justice and to understanding the conditions necessary for a healthy political order. In both *Walden* and, even more astutely, his later essay "Life Without Principle," Thoreau diagnoses the diseases to which those who follow the news too closely are prone.

Thoreau warns that the increased abundance and speed of the news threaten to fragment our attention and damage our ability to see what is really happening and to think rightly about these events. As Josef Pieper puts it, in making a parallel argument, "The average person of our time loses the ability to see because *there is too much to see!*"[1] Even worse, when so many voices vie for our attention, they have to get louder and more sensational to gain a hearing; fake news, sensationalized headlines that today would be labeled "clickbait," and yellow

---

[1]Josef Pieper, *Only the Lover Sings: Art and Contemplation*, trans. Lothar Krauth (San Francisco: Ignatius Press, 1990), 32 (emphasis original).

journalism all developed in the nineteenth century.[2] In response to this unhealthy environment, Thoreau devoted his attention to what he called "the Eternities" and cautioned against the dangers of being swept up in the flurry created by the news industry. In particular, I'll enumerate three symptoms Thoreau thinks result from this fragmented attention—what he calls a "macadamized" intellect. First, it induces a vague, underlying sense of boredom and dis-ease, what he terms a mental "dyspepsia." Second, it renders us vulnerable to the wiles of advertisers and politicians. And third, it warps our emotional sensibilities, directing them toward distant, spectacular events and making it more difficult for us to sympathize with and love our neighbors.

Before we get to Thoreau's diagnosis, though, we need a bit of context about the technological changes he experienced. The printing presses used in colonial America were not much different from the one that Gutenberg used in fifteenth-century Germany, but between 1800 and 1840 printing technology advanced rapidly: first came iron presses, then the steam-powered Adams press and steam-powered rotary presses, then stereotyping and electrotyping. Alongside these improvements, steam-powered paper mills and new methods of producing paper from wood fiber dramatically decreased the cost of paper.[3] Furthermore, other nineteenth-century technologies

---

[2]Alex Boese, *The Museum of Hoaxes: A History of Outrageous Pranks and Deceptions* (New York: Plume, 2003); David R. Spencer, *The Yellow Journalism: The Press and America's Emergence as a World Power* (Evanston, IL: Northwestern University Press, 2007); and Kevin Young, *Bunk: The Rise of Hoaxes, Humbug, Plagiarists, Phonies, Post-Facts, and Fake News* (Minneapolis: Graywolf Press, 2017).

[3]As Louis Dudek writes, "Gutenberg's invention (printing from moveable types) has absorbed all the dramatic attention of historians. . . . But since 1800, the Industrial Revolution in Printing, far more overwhelming in its effects, in fact the true determinant of our present culture, has been virtually neglected." Louis Dudek, *Literature and the Press: A History of Printing, Printed Media, and Their Relation to Literature* (Toronto: Ryerson Press, 1960), 9. See also Scott E.

transformed the nation's communication infrastructure: the telegraph, the railroad, and photography shrank the world dramatically. Indeed, the difference between words printed by hand and carried by horse or sail and words printed by steam and carried by wires or rails may well be as vast as the difference between nineteenth-century technologies and twenty-first-century digital technologies.

Visitors to the 1876 Centennial Exhibition in Philadelphia had a vivid display of these technological improvements. In a speech given to the American Book Trade Association, which held its annual meeting in conjunction with the exhibition, the chairman of the reception committee highlighted a display in Machinery Hall. There, visitors could see

> the old printing-press of Franklin, upon which, by hard labor he could produce perhaps 150 impressions per hour, side by side with the Messrs. Hoe & Co.'s latest invention, the Web perfecting-press, printing 32,000 copies of a newspaper, on both sides, in the same time. . . . Steam, the telegraph, and the power printing-press, what have they not accomplished, and how have they changed the condition of the civilized world![4]

A 42,666 percent increase in efficiency is quite remarkable, and those who lived through these changes acutely felt this disruptive power.

Casper, Jeffrey D. Groves, Stephen W. Nissenbaum, and Michael Winship, eds., *The Industrial Book, 1840–1880*, vol. 3 of *A History of the Book in America* (Chapel Hill: University of North Carolina Press, 2007); Robert A. Gross and Mary Kelley, eds., *An Extensive Republic: Print, Culture, and Society in the New Nation, 1790–1840*, vol. 2 of *A History of the Book in America* (Chapel Hill: University of North Carolina Press, 2014); and Robert Hoe, *A Short History of the Printing Press and of the Improvements in Printing Machinery from the Time of Gutenberg up to the Present Day (1902)* (New York: Robert Hoe, 1902).
[4]J. B. Mitchell, "Address of Welcome," *Publishers Weekly* 10 (1876): 167. For a discussion of the American Book Trade Association and this meeting, see Casper et al., *Industrial Book, 1840–1880*, 1.

These technological developments—and the economic shifts they made possible—led to the kind of news-as-spectacle that is so prevalent today. As Neil Postman argues, these nineteenth-century technologies ushered in "the Age of Show Business."[5] At times Postman evinces a naive confidence in the unalloyed goods of print, but he recognizes that these industrial technologies mark an important inflection point. And in the wake of these changes, more and more Americans came to realize that technological advances don't necessarily foster moral growth; in fact, they can introduce new temptations and dangers.

The Macadamizing Process

It was in this context that Thoreau wrote his lecture "Life Without Principle" as a sort of follow-up to *Walden*. He gave versions of it repeatedly over the last decade of his life, and it was published posthumously in the *Atlantic*. The lecture is a critique of industrial standards of value, and Thoreau invites his hearers to "consider the way in which we spend our lives," measuring our lives not by quantitative or monetary standards but by whether we live up to our stated principles.[6] The lecture's second half in particular focuses on how we spend our attention, and Thoreau pulls no punches in describing the dangers that the industrialized news industry poses to a principled life.

Drawing on biblical imagery, Thoreau warns his hearers that newspapers can become idols. An obsession with the distractions of the daily paper can reveal an inattention—even an infidelity—to the ongoing work of the Creator. As Thoreau puts it,

---

[5]Neil Postman, *Amusing Ourselves to Death: Public Discourse in the Age of Show Business* (New York: Penguin, 1986), 63.

[6]Henry David Thoreau, *Reform Papers*, ed. Wendell Glick, Writings of Henry David Thoreau (Princeton, NJ: Princeton University Press, 1973), 156.

I do not know but it is too much to read one newspaper a week. I have tried it recently, and for so long it seems to me that I have not dwelt in my native region. The sun, the clouds, the snow, the trees say not so much to me. You cannot serve two masters. It requires more than a day's devotion to know and to possess the wealth of a day.[7]

Thoreau then moves from Jesus' warning against serving mammon (Mt 6:24 KJV) to Paul's sermon at the Areopagus where he tells the Athenians to stop worshiping idols and instead serve God because "in him we live and move and have our being" (Acts 17:28). Thoreau claims that the news competes with this God, offering an alternative, secular ground of being: "If you chance to live and move and have your being in that thin stratum in which the events that make the news transpire— thinner than the paper on which it is printed—then these things will fill the world for you; but if you soar above or dive below that plane, you cannot remember nor be reminded of them."[8] What we attend to reveals and shapes our loves, so if our attention is fixed on the thin stratum of the daily news, then we are guilty of a kind of idolatry, of misdirecting our love and even worship. Thoreau's warning against idolatry is seconded by Simone Weil, an early twentieth-century French polymath and mystic, who claims "the habit of . . . attention . . . is the substance of prayer."[9]

This link between attention and worship or love may seem tenuous, but as the etymology of the word suggests, *attention* entails a deep mutuality or reciprocity that is at the root of love. To attend to something means literally "to stretch toward" it.

[7]Ibid., 169.
[8]Ibid., 170.
[9]Simone Weil, *Waiting for God*, trans. Emma Craufurd (New York: Harper & Row, 1973), 108.

The English words *tension, tune,* and *tend* all come from the same Indo-European root meaning "to stretch." *Tend* itself carries a dual meaning that speaks to the nuances embedded in this notion of stretching: "to tend" means both to move toward something, a tendency, and to care for something, to tend a garden, say. So *attention* signifies a relation stretched between two different things. And embedded in the connotations of these related words—to tend to another or to be in tune with another—is the suggestion of propriety in this stretching. When attention is exercised properly, a certain harmonious resonance comes into existence. So while attention maintains a difference between subject and object, we do tend to become more like that which we attend to: we become what we love.[10] It is impossible, then, to attend deeply to something and not be changed.[11]

It is this transformative power of attention that leads Thoreau to a startling and profound metaphor. He claims that attending to the trivia of the news *macadamizes* our intellect. This is a term for a method of road construction named after its inventor, John McAdam, a Scottish engineer. While most roads were built on a foundation of large stones, McAdam used small, hand-broken stones to surface roads; supervisors actually measured the stones to be sure that no large ones slipped through. The angular edges of these rocks would bind together and form a smooth, long-lasting surface for traffic. McAdam's name lives on today in the word *tarmac*, which refers to macadam roads that were sprayed with tar to cut the dust. With

---

[10]This insight forms the title of an excellent book that charts the power of our habits to form our loves: James K. A. Smith, *You Are What You Love: The Spiritual Power of Habit* (Grand Rapids, MI: Brazos Press, 2016).

[11]This paragraph is drawn from my work on Wendell Berry's poetry and its portrayal of attention: Jeffrey Bilbro, *Virtues of Renewal: Wendell Berry's Sustainable Forms* (Lexington: University Press of Kentucky, 2019), 30.

Figure 1.1. *The First Macadam Road*, 1823, by Carl Rakeman

that bit of background, here's Thoreau's description of how patterns of attention can alter our minds:

> I believe that the mind can be permanently profaned by the habit of attending to trivial things, so that all our thoughts shall be tinged with triviality. Our very intellect shall be macadamized, as it were—its foundation broken into fragments for the wheels of travel to roll over; and if you would know what will make the most durable pavement, surpassing rolled stones, spruce blocks, and asphaltum, you have only to look into some of our minds which have been subjected to this treatment so long.[12]

Thoreau weaves together several key terms in these two sentences. To begin with, *profaned* compares our minds to temples.

---

[12]Thoreau, *Reform Papers*, 173.

Fane is the Latin word for "temple," so *profane* literally means "before or outside the temple." When we attend too closely to secular, temporal affairs, we "desecrate" our minds. Hence Thoreau goes on to say in the following sentence that we should "make once more a fane of the mind." There are lasting, even eternal, consequences for what we give our attention to. This is why Paul instructs the Colossians to "set your minds on things that are above, not on things that are on earth" (Col 3:2).

Habit emphasizes the repetitive, formative nature of attention. Thoreau's life and writings certainly demonstrate his own knowledge of contemporary events, so he's not advocating that we hole ourselves up and ignore everything that's going on around us.[13] After all, Thoreau himself helped runaway slaves, participated in abolitionist movements, and spent a night in jail over his refusal to pay a tax that would have helped fund the Mexican-American War. Such social engagement flowed not from an obsession with the news of the day but from his commitment to eternal, moral truths. Thus Thoreau is urging us to reflect on our habits, our patterns of attention that shape and fill our minds. What does our daily reading look like? What do we turn to when we're bored? These are the habits of attention that shape our souls.

Trivia is of course an indictment of the frivolous affairs that populate the news, but this word also continues Thoreau's road metaphor. *Trivia* comes from a Latin word meaning "an intersection of three roads," so by implication it refers to a place that

---

[13]While Thoreau is sometimes accused of withdrawing from society, Laura Dassow Walls's masterful biography demonstrates this is an unfair caricature. Laura Dassow Walls, *Henry David Thoreau: A Life* (Chicago: University of Chicago Press, 2017). For a particularly egregious example of a misreading of Thoreau, see Kathryn Schulz, "The Moral Judgments of Henry David Thoreau," *New Yorker*, October 12, 2015, www.newyorker.com/magazine/2015/10/19/pond-scum.

is well traveled. In English, it came to refer to things that were common, well known, and hence insignificant. Thoreau nods to these roots when he writes earlier in this paragraph, "If I am to be a thoroughfare, I prefer that it be of the mountain-brooks, the Parnassian streams, and not the town-sewers."[14] Thoreau imagines our minds as conduits or roadways for ideas, and we are responsible to choose what we want rolling down these streets. Yet, when we habitually attend to trivial things, our minds turn into gravel and become susceptible to whatever ads or slogans or memes other people send spinning down our macadamized intellects.

In his lecture, Thoreau goes on to propose a two-part remedy for this condition:

> If we have thus desecrated ourselves,—as who has not?— the remedy will be by wariness and devotion to reconsecrate ourselves, and make once more a fane of the mind. We should treat our minds, that is, ourselves, as innocent and ingenuous children, whose guardians we are, and be careful what objects and what subjects we thrust on their attention. Read not the Times. Read the Eternities.[15]

As Thoreau acknowledges, we have all, to one degree or another, desecrated our minds by attending to trivia, but Thoreau hopes that by (1) wariness and (2) devotion we can reconsecrate our minds and make them into temples or fanes again. If the problem is habitual attention to things outside the temple, the solution is habitual attention to things inside the temple. This is a two-part movement: it's a movement away from the gossip and trivia of the Times and a movement toward the good, beautiful, complex truth of the Eternities.

---

[14]Thoreau, *Reform Papers*, 172.
[15]Ibid., 173.

Again, despite his strident rhetoric here, Thoreau is not advocating absolute withdrawal from the affairs of time. This is not a head-in-the-sand denialism. Rather, Thoreau insists that insofar as we are formed by the ephemeral dramas and scandals of the daily news, we will be unable to contribute meaningfully and redemptively to the real issues and concerns of our times. We will simply be passive highways for the trends and outrage that populate our news feeds.

While Thoreau didn't have twenty-first-century research about the brain to support his claims that our habits of attention have long-lasting effects, recent scholarship backs up his metaphor. As we become increasingly embedded in an "ecosystem of interruption technologies" that fosters a state of "continuous partial attention," our neural networks are actually being restructured.[16] Books like Susan Greenfield's *Mind Change: How Digital Technologies Are Leaving Their Mark on Our Brains* and Nicholas Carr's *The Shallows: What the Internet Is Doing to Our Brains* chart the work of neuroscientists who are discovering the incredible plasticity of our brains.[17] We can indeed macadamize our intellects by attending to trivia. In the next chapter, we'll flesh out the contours of the healthier posture Thoreau recommends, but in the remainder of this chapter I'll examine in a bit more detail three effects or symptoms of a macadamized mind.

---

[16]Cory Doctorow, "Writing in the Age of Distraction," *Locus Magazine*, January 2009, www.locusmag.com/Features/2009/01/cory-doctorow-writing-in-age-of.html; Linda Stone, "Continuous Partial Attention," November 30, 2009, https://lindastone.net/2009/11/30/beyond-simple-multi-tasking-continuous-partial-attention; both quoted in Alan Jacobs, "Habits of Mind in an Age of Distraction," *Comment*, June 1, 2016, 38-46.

[17]Susan Greenfield, *Mind Change: How Digital Technologies Are Leaving Their Mark on Our Brains* (New York: Random House, 2015); and Nicholas Carr, *The Shallows: What the Internet Is Doing to Our Brains* (New York: Norton, 2011).

Mental Dyspepsia

At the conclusion of "Life Without Principle," Thoreau shifts metaphorical registers and compares the act of attention to that of eating. If we attend to unhealthy news, we—as both individuals and communities—can get a kind of indigestion:

> Those things which now most engage the attention of men, as politics and the daily routine, are, it is true, vital functions of human society, but should be unconsciously performed, like the corresponding functions of the physical body. . . . Not only individuals, but States, have thus a confirmed dyspepsia, which expresses itself, you can imagine by what sort of eloquence. Thus our life is not altogether a forgetting, but also, alas! to a great extent, a remembering, of that which we should never have been conscious of, certainly not in our waking hours.[18]

Thoreau's vivid imagery—or perhaps I should say his pungent olfactory description—conveys the dangers of indiscriminate consumption of the news. An unhealthy mental diet results in a kind of intellectual bloating and discomfort, and the problem is further compounded because such a diet intensifies our craving for mental junk food. This is not just an individual problem; Thoreau points out that states too can suffer the dyspeptic effects of fragmented attention. Politics in the age of Twitter bears out his warnings.

Thoreau calls this disordered intellectual appetite *curiosity*. It's analogous to a craving for snacks that are salty or sweet but lack real nutrition. And the more we give in to this craving, the less we are able to resist it: "In proportion as our inward life fails, we go more constantly and desperately to

---

[18]Thoreau, *Reform Papers*, 178-79.

the post-office. . . . In health we have not the least curiosity about such events. We do not live for idle amusement. I would not run round a corner to see the world blow up."[19] Attending to titillating ephemera creates a vicious cycle as our "inward life fails" and we become further enslaved to the whims of our curiosity.[20]

It is this disordered appetite that explains why we watch cat videos on YouTube and share memes on Facebook when we have access to what Thoreau calls "the treasured wealth of the world."[21] This is why more people take *BuzzFeed* quizzes than read long-form essays in the *Atlantic*. It's why we itch to check Facebook or Instagram every five minutes. It is always more tempting to eat candy and fast food instead of fresh vegetables from the garden. It's easier to get an emotional "hit" from shallow, sensational news than it is to spend the mental energy required to engage with more serious matters; watching the world blow up is more exciting than studying its treasured wealth.

This is an old problem: humans have always been tempted to rubbernecking and gossip. But just as junk food poses new threats when food engineers find ways to make it maximally addictive, so the news industry preys on our inherent disposition to curiosity through ever more sophisticated techniques. Advanced analytics enable website editors to identify the traits that are likely to make a story go viral, and they use this

---

[19]Ibid., 169-70.

[20]Thoreau's critique of curiosity parallels, in some respects, Augustine's theological taxonomy of intellectual appetites. Paul J. Griffiths, *Intellectual Appetite: A Theological Grammar* (Washington, DC: Catholic University of America Press, 2009).

[21]Henry David Thoreau, *Walden and Civil Disobedience* (New York: Penguin Classics, 1983), 148. For more on this problem, see Jean M. Twenge, *IGen: Why Today's Super-Connected Kids Are Growing Up Less Rebellious, More Tolerant, Less Happy—and Completely Unprepared for Adulthood—and What That Means for the Rest of Us* (New York: Simon & Schuster, 2017), 66.

information to choose what news to cover and to hone clickbait headlines that will entice more revenue-generating clicks.[22] We can't simply blame journalists for these developments: existential economic pressures lead newsrooms to adopt such tactics, and they wouldn't be effective if readers demanded more substantive fare.

The irony is that when we succumb to these temptations, we are not satiated. Instead, we get that bloated feeling that has led people to talk about "binging" on Netflix. Thoreau didn't have streaming TV to critique, so his targets are the "profane and stale revelation of the bar-room and the police court"—he wouldn't be impressed with *CSI* and its spinoffs—and the wildly popular sentimental novels.[23] In *Walden*, he upbraids his neighbors who "with saucer eyes, and erect and primitive curiosity, and with unwearied gizzard" gorge themselves on the latest installment from the pen of their favored novelist.[24] "To read well," Thoreau writes, "is a noble exercise, and one that will task the reader more than any exercise which the customs of the day esteem."[25] Hence, he urges his neighbors to feed their minds on a more robust diet than can be found in "the columns of the daily paper."[26]

Thoreau's rigorous standards can make him seem like a tiresome scold. After all, isn't there something to be said for unwinding after a long day by watching some TV or scrolling through our news feed? Perhaps, but Thoreau's dietary metaphor contains an important insight. Some modes of relaxation—much like "comfort food"—actually *keep* us in a state of

---

[22]Nicole Blanchett Neheli, "Here's How Metrics and Analytics Are Changing Newsroom Practice," *JSource*, February 20, 2019, https://j-source.ca/article/heres-how-metrics-and-analytics-are-changing-newsroom-practice/.

[23]Thoreau, *Reform Papers*, 172.

[24]Thoreau, *Walden*, 150.

[25]Ibid., 146.

[26]Ibid., 153.

bloated exhaustion. The ennui that leads us to binge watch Netflix or mindlessly scroll through a social media feed, looking for easy tidbits of emotional excitement, is a result of overstimulation and indiscriminate news consumption. So, paradoxically, we may be less tired and have more mental energy if we shut up the doors of our fane and discipline our attention.

An older, Christian term for the kind of appetite that results in this dyspepsia is *acedia*, what the desert fathers called "the noonday devil."[27] Acedia manifests as indifference or listlessness regarding substantive, eternal matters—we find it difficult to attend to what we should. So we flit from headline to headline, skimming in search of some new outrage or drama. This condition is the intellectual corollary to what William Cavanaugh describes in writing about the ironies of consumeristic materialism: "What really characterizes consumer culture is not attachment to things but detachment. . . . People do not cling to things; they discard them and buy other things."[28] Cavanaugh's analysis of consumerism needs just a few substituted phrases to apply to the condition of disordered attention: "Our relationships with [news stories] tend to be short-lived: rather than [pondering important developments], consumers are characterized by a constant dissatisfaction with [what they've just read]. This dissatisfaction is what produces the restless pursuit of satisfaction in the form of something new."[29] For all our hunger for the next bit of breaking news, we quickly forget

[27]Nault Jean-Charles, *The Noonday Devil: Acedia, the Unnamed Evil of Our Times* (San Francisco: Ignatius Press, 2015). I've written elsewhere about the poet Richard Wilbur's description of and remedy for acedia, or what he terms a "fierce velleity." Jeffrey Bilbro, "Fierce Velleity: Poetry as Antidote to Acedia," *Front Porch Republic*, February 20, 2019, www.frontporchrepublic.com/2019/02/fierce-velleity/.

[28]William T. Cavanaugh, *Being Consumed: Economics and Christian Desire* (Grand Rapids, MI: Eerdmans, 2008), 34.

[29]Ibid., 35.

it once we've extracted the emotional charge it can give us. We are soon hungry for the next outrage, the next unbelievable headline, the next political scandal. We have an intense desire to know *something*, but the object of that desire remains indeterminate and vague. So we scroll hurriedly through our news feed looking for something to latch onto. The desert fathers knew that discipline is the only cure for such a condition, and Thoreau agrees: "By all kinds of traps and sign-boards, threatening the extreme penalty of the divine law, exclude such trespassers from the only ground which can be sacred to you. It is so hard to forget what it is worse than useless to remember!"[30]

Passive Thoroughfare

This restless curiosity, this craving for some new bit of entertainment, makes us incredibly vulnerable to the wiles of advertisers and politicians and ideologues. We become susceptible to the latest groupthink because our thoughts are dictated by trending jargon or viral hashtags. To return to Thoreau's core metaphor, a macadamized mind, an intellect ground to bits and made into a highway offers little resistance to whatever thought or emotion is driven down it. Hence, we become passive thoroughfares, the objects of our attention determined by whatever headlines or memes happen to be going viral.

If our intellects are macadamized, we actually lack the vocabulary or categories to see the world truthfully. We'll simply take in the events around us through the prepackaged categories provided by the mass media. In his brief essay "Learning How to See Again," Pieper identifies this problem and asks, "How can man be saved from becoming a totally passive consumer of mass-produced goods and a subservient follower

---

[30]Thoreau, *Reform Papers*, 172.

beholden to every slogan the managers may proclaim?" This is a serious challenge because the passive consumer, the subservient follower, "inevitably falls prey to the demagogical spells of any powers that be."[31] Pieper's remedy, which I'll return to in chapter three, is to develop an artistic craft, but it's his acute identification of this problem that is most relevant here.

Hashtags and slogans lack the precision and nuance required to do justice to the complexity of our world and time. If these are the only tools we have, we will be unable to make adequate sense of the news. The agrarian writer Wendell Berry extends Thoreau's argument in his essay "In Defense of Literacy," arguing that America's education system has failed to give students the robust language required to think carefully in a culture that is inundated with persuasive statements urging us to buy this or think that. Berry claims that when we acquiesce to "the doctrine that the purpose of education is the mass production of producers and consumers," we tend to treat literacy as an ornamental add-on. Berry warns, however, that "we will understand the world, and preserve ourselves and our values in it, only insofar as we have a language that is alert and responsive to it, and careful of it." He goes on to name our danger precisely: "In our society, which exists in an atmosphere of prepared, public language . . . illiteracy is both a personal and a public danger." This is because we are "forever being asked to buy or believe somebody else's line of goods. The line of goods is being sold, moreover, by men who are trained to make him buy it or believe it, whether or not he needs it or understands it or knows its value or wants it."[32]

---

[31]Pieper, *Only the Lover Sings*, 33-34.
[32]Wendell Berry, "In Defense of Literacy," in *A Continuous Harmony: Essays Cultural and Agricultural* (San Diego: Harcourt Brace, 1972), 169-71.

An education system that has been co-opted by career training means that more and more of us are unable to navigate what is an increasingly hazardous verbal environment. And our fragmented habits of attention exacerbate this problem: "An unmixed diet" of shallow, transient language,

> language meant to be replaced by what will immediately follow it, . . . is destructive of the informed, resilient, critical intelligence that the best of our traditions have sought to create and to maintain. . . . Such intelligence does not grow by bloating upon the ephemeral information and misinformation of the public media. It grows by returning again and again to the landmarks of its cultural birthright, the works that have proved worthy of attention.[33]

It is here that Berry cites Thoreau's prescription: "Read not the Times. Read the Eternities." Chewing on rich wisdom articulated in careful language feeds our minds and enables us to discern the nuances of the events happening in our time. If we want to exercise more responsibility regarding what ideas we entertain, we will need to develop the attention and vocabulary required to relate truthfully to a complex world. Or, as Berry puts it, "We must speak, and teach our children to speak, a language precise and articulate and lively enough to tell the truth about the world as we know it."[34] And we won't learn this language if our minds have become passive thoroughfares for advertising jingles, political slogans, and hashtags.

---

[33]Ibid., 172-73.
[34]Ibid. Elsewhere, Jack Baker and I develop the implications that Berry's understanding of language has for education. Jack R. Baker and Jeffrey Bilbro, *Wendell Berry and Higher Education: Cultivating Virtues of Place*, Culture of the Land (Lexington: University Press of Kentucky, 2017), 47-69.

Hacking at the Branches

When we habitually attend to distant news, it's not just our minds that are damaged; we become less able to feel and act responsibly. In *Walden*, where he also warns readers of the dangers of obsessive news consumption, Thoreau describes this problem by critiquing the recent boom in philanthropic activity: "There are a thousand hacking at the branches of evil to one who is striking at the root, and it may be that he who bestows the largest amount of time and money on the needy is doing the most by his mode of life to produce that misery which he strives in vain to relieve."[35] Thoreau's polemic against the "drastic philanthropy [that] seeks out the Esquimaux and the Patagonian" is famously echoed in fictional form by Charles Dickens's character Mrs. Jellyby. A minor character in *Bleak House*, Mrs. Jellyby is a "telescopic philanthropist" fixated on helping people in Africa while blithely neglecting her own children.[36] In our twenty-first-century media ecosystem, we are all in danger of becoming Mrs. Jellybys: making the news media the primary lens through which we view the world magnifies the significance of distant, shocking events and obscures the important events happening at hand.

News-as-spectacle, whether a political scandal, a natural disaster, a terrorist attack, or almost any story as rendered by television, shapes those who consume it to be passive spectators. As Eitan Hersh explains, summarizing a Pew Research

---

[35]Thoreau, *Walden*, 119. For a history of American philanthropy—and a critique of the turn it took in the nineteenth century—see Jeremy Beer, *The Philanthropic Revolution: An Alternative History of American Charity* (Philadelphia: University of Pennsylvania Press, 2015).

[36]Charles Dickens, *Bleak House* (Oxford: Oxford University Press, 1998), 44-57. Adam Gurri borrows Dickens's metaphor for his analysis of "telescopic morality." Adam Gurri, "Free Yourself from the Telescopic Morality Machine," *Front Porch Republic*, December 9, 2014, www.frontporchrepublic.com/2014/12 /free-telescopic-morality-machine/.

Center study, "Daily news consumers are very interested in politics, so they say, but they aren't doing much: In 2016 most reported belonging to zero organizations, having attended zero political meetings in the last year, having worked zero times with others to solve a community problem."[37] If we do manage to find some way of acting in response to the latest gripping news event, it tends to be through a kind of dramatic gesture—donating to a celebrity's foundation or posting a video of someone dumping ice water over us—that aims at distant symptoms rather than nearby causes.[38] Yet the stories that fill the news foster the erroneous belief that we have to feel intensely about, and do what we can to address, the most visible and spectacular problems rather than attend to—and tend to—nearby issues. When our experience of the world is filtered through the news media, the tragedies that play out on our screens can seem more pressing than the ones that happen closer to home. In this condition, we risk being like the priest and the Levite, who passed by the wounded man on the side of the road, rather than the Samaritan, who saw, had compassion for, and took action to help his neighbor (Lk 10:25-37).

As Jesus' parable indicates, telescopic or misdirected attention, and the disordered love that follows, isn't a new problem. Nonetheless, improvements in communications technology have increased the temptation to sympathize with distant events and ignore ones nearby. It's no accident that Thoreau and Dickens addressed this problem in the mid-nineteenth century. Thoreau fingered the telegraph as part of

---

[37]Eitan Hersh, "College-Educated Voters Are Ruining American Politics," *Atlantic*, January 20, 2020, www.theatlantic.com/ideas/archive/2020/01/political-hobbyists-are-ruining-politics/605212/.

[38]"Ice Bucket Challenge," in *Wikipedia, the Free Encyclopedia*, accessed July 20, 2020, https://en.wikipedia.org/w/index.php?title=Ice_Bucket_Challenge&oldid=732524020.

the problem, and he quipped that once the transatlantic telegraph cable was finally laid, "perchance the first news that will
leak through into the broad, flapping American ear will be
that the Princess Adelaide has the whooping cough."[39] Neil
Postman agrees with Thoreau that this technology inaugurated many of the problematic dynamics associated with the
modern news industry: "Only four years after Morse opened
the nation's first telegraph line on May 24, 1844, the Associated Press was founded, and news from nowhere, addressed
to no one in particular, began to crisscross the nation. Wars,
crimes, crashes, fires, floods—much of it the social and political equivalent of Adelaide's whooping cough—became the
content of what people called 'the news of the day.'" Thus
Postman claims that the telegraph "dramatically altered what
may be called the 'information-action ratio.'"[40] By flooding us
with information to which we can have no meaningful response, these technologies threaten to malform our affective
sensibilities. The goal of a properly attentive life is right love
and right action, and this goal is not served when we are
caught up in distant dramas.

The contemporary novelist Barbara Kingsolver, in a marvelous essay detailing why she and her family don't watch TV,
describes a conversation she had with a friend about the air-
plane crash involving John Kennedy Jr. Kingsolver writes that
she hadn't heard the news because she had been "attending
only to the news of my own community" for several weeks, and
her friend was shocked that she didn't know about this tragedy.
Yet Kingsolver averred that "it would make no real difference
in my life":

---

[39]Thoreau, *Walden*, 95-96.
[40]Postman, *Amusing Ourselves to Death*, 67-68.

It's not that I'm callous about the calamities suffered by famous people; they are heartaches, to be sure, but heartaches genuinely experienced only by their own friends and families. It seems somewhat voyeuristic, and also absurd, to expect that JFK Jr.'s death should change my life any more than a recent death in *my* family affected the Kennedys. . . . On the matter of individual tragic deaths, I believe that those in my own neighborhood are the ones I need to attend to first, by means of casseroles and whatever else I can offer. I also believe it's possible to be so overtaken and stupefied by the tragedies of the world that we don't have any time or energy left for those closer to home, the hurts we should take as our own.[41]

Kingsolver's attitude here parallels Thoreau's, and she wisely insists on directing her emotional energy toward people and events to which she can lovingly respond. As Augustine advises, "All people should be loved equally. But you cannot do good to all people equally, so you should take particular thought for those who, as if by lot, happen to be particularly close to you in terms of place, time, or any other circumstances."[42]

Near the end of Thoreau's "Life Without Principle," he stubbornly declares, "I have not got to answer for having read a single President's Message."[43] Yet when the news is filled with breathless analysis of the latest presidential tweet, it makes us imagine that we must somehow respond to every dispatch from the White House. We don't! What would such a response even look like? In most cases, any imaginable reply would amount to

[41]Barbara Kingsolver, "The One-Eyed Monster, and Why I Don't Let Him In," in *Small Wonder: Essays* (New York: HarperCollins, 2009), 142.

[42]Augustine, *On Christian Teaching*, trans. R. P. H. Green (Oxford: Oxford University Press, 2008), 21.

[43]Thoreau, *Reform Papers*, 177.

hacking at the branches of the problem while our mode of life—for instance, our own complicity in a news-entertainment complex that profits from politicians who churn out new scandals every hour—perpetuates a spectacle-driven politics. Habitually attending to the trivia of the day macadamizes our intellects, gives us mental dyspepsia, makes us vulnerable to groupthink, and deforms our affective responses. The result of all this is that we are less able to attend to and love our neighbors.

MANY NEWS STORIES AREN'T. ACTUALLY, ABLE TO AFFECT OUR LIVES. SO, WHY WASTE THE PRECIOUS TIME, WHEN WE SHOULD PAY MORE ATTENTION OR LOVE OUR FAMILY & NEIGHBORS?

REBECCA

Chapter Two

The Blessed Man as a Rooted Tree

IN 1933, AS HITLER'S Nazi party rose to power in Germany, the Jewish artist Marc Chagall painted *Solitude*. In the foreground, a seated man sits wrapped in a tallit, or prayer shawl. His right hand supports his head in an attitude of contemplation, and his left arm embraces a large Torah scroll. At his side, a heifer seems to be playing a violin.[1] In the background the city of Vitebsk—where Chagall was born and raised—is shrouded in darkness and watched over by an angel. At the time he painted this, Chagall was working "obsessively" on a commission to illustrate the Old Testament while also keenly aware of the looming clouds of Nazi anti-Semitism.[2] Indeed, one of the Nazis' first examples of "degenerate" Jewish art was a painting by Chagall.

In the midst of these unsettling political developments, Chagall drew on the Jewish tradition of deep, loving attention to the Scripture. The violin-playing cow is an image of the imaginative, artistic meditation on the divine Word being practiced by the man cradling the Torah scroll. Why a cow? Because the Hebrew word *hagah*, like the Latinate English word *ruminate*,

[1] Mira Friedman, "Marc Chagall's Portrayal of the Prophet Jeremiah," *Zeitschrift für Kunstgeschichte* 47, no. 3 (1984): 384-86.
[2] Jackie Wullschlager, *Chagall: A Biography* (New York: Knopf, 2008), 353.

Figure 2.1. *Solitude*, 1933, by Marc Chagall

means both "to meditate" and also "to chew the cud." David Jeffrey links Chagall's painting to this trope, explaining that "by analogy with the peaceable heifer, a spiritually flourishing person is said to be one who meditates on the Word of God, day and night."[3] One of the iconic Old Testament passages that relies on this wordplay is Psalm 1, where the blessed man "delight[s] in the law of the LORD, / and on his law he meditates day and night" (Ps 1:2). The result of this meditation is not just some kind of personal enrichment: the psalmist compares the person who ruminates on God's Word to a tree "planted by streams of water / that yields its fruit in its season, / and its leaf does not wither" (Ps 1:3). The result of scriptural rumination is fruit that blesses one's place and community. The rooted life of the blessed man contrasts with "the wicked [who] . . . / are like the chaff that the wind drives away" (Ps 1:4). These chafflike

---

[3]David Lyle Jeffrey, *In the Beauty of Holiness: Art and the Bible in Western Culture* (Grand Rapids, MI: Eerdmans, 2017), 332-33.

fools are blown about by the latest fads and trends; in this way, they are like those with macadamized minds. A Christian image for healthy attention, then, might be this rooted tree—or a violin-playing heifer.

In Chagall's painting, the meditative figure is not ignoring the events of his time and place in order to lose himself in solipsistic, irrelevant flights of fancy. Rather, he is feeding on the eternal truths most needed in this turbulent historical moment. As one of Chagall's biographers notes, this painting is part of Chagall's own response "to the omens heralding the destruction of the world that had nourished him."[4] Crucially, in the background of the painting an angel—suggesting divine providence— is watching over human affairs even when they seem imponderably dark to human eyes. Chagall's composition suggests that trust in Providence and an imaginative attention to the Word of God provide the proper perspective from which to view the events of our day.

Chagall's seated figure gestures toward a kind of contemplative politics, to use a phrase that may seem paradoxical. A contemplative politics entails a two-part movement, one that parallels Thoreau's injunction to be *wary* of trivia and *devoted* to eternal truths. The first involves an askesis, a kind of self-discipline, that refuses attention to the buzzing alerts and urgent headlines that threaten to macadamize our minds. A helpful guide in this endeavor is the French mathematician and theologian Blaise Pascal, who shows how a confidence in God's providence can free us from seeing the news as a series of reports on existential crises and can enable us to cultivate a holy apathy, a *sancta indifferentia*, toward this temporal frenzy. The second movement entails loving action rooted in contemplation

---

[4]Wullschlager, *Chagall*, 357.

of God and his Word. The twentieth-century Trappist monk Thomas Merton serves as a helpful example in this regard; he detached himself from the daily scrum in order to devote himself more deeply to a few particularly important issues such as race relations and interreligious dialogue. And his work on these subjects flowed from prayerful contemplation of Scripture and God's presence. Loving attention to the divine Word should result in profound love for those with whom we share our place and time. As C. S. Lewis remarks, "If you read history you will find that the Christians who did most for the present world were just those who thought most of the next."[5]

Sancta Indifferentia

In the mid-seventeenth century, Blaise Pascal wrote a letter to his brother-in-law in which he reflected on the nature of political controversies. His recommendations are broadly applicable to the way in which we engage the myriad social and political dramas that fill the news. Pascal's brother-in-law wrote him about a controversy in which he was involved, and Pascal replied by sketching a view of Providence as guiding not only our efforts but also those of our opponents: "The same Providence that has inspired some with light, has refused it to others."[6] In other words, the God that allows you to have the right perspective on this particular issue also allows others to be wrong about it. Recognizing that the outcome of all our controversies is in God's hand—that in some sense he wills or permits people to hold different views on these issues—should radically temper our emotional investment in the victory of our

---

[5]C. S. Lewis, *Mere Christianity* (San Francisco: HarperOne, 2015), 134.
[6]Blaise Pascal, *Blaise Pascal: Thoughts, Letters, Minor Works*, trans. W. F. Trotter, M. L. Booth, and O. W. Wight, Harvard Classics 48 (New York: P. F. Collier & Son, 1910), 343.

preferred side. Such a recognition would certainly dampen the fury with which Christians all too often fight "culture wars."

In part, Pascal's stance flows from an epistemic humility: we may be misguided in our perception of what the right course of action is in a given situation. But more than that, Pascal thinks that even if we are advocating for a political or social cause that is in line with God's will, we must remember that God himself allows others to oppose us: "The same motive power which leads us to act, leads others to resist us, or permits them at least." Pascal pushes this even further, claiming, "It is much more certain that God permits the evil, however great it may be, than that God causes the good in us (and not some secret motive)."[7] We can be more certain that God wills opposition to our preferred causes than that we ourselves are being motivated by God. This is a sobering thought.

In fact, Pascal goes on to suggest that the most reliable marker of whether we are motivated by God lies in our equanimity in the face of opposition: if "we suffer external hindrances with patience, this signifies that there is a uniformity of will between the motive power that inspires our passions and the one that permits the resistance to them; and as there is no doubt that it is God who permits the one, we have a right humbly to hope that it is God who produces the other."[8] The upshot, then, is that Pascal recommends a profound sort of apathy, a *sancta indifferentia*, toward the outcome of the issues we read about and advocate for.

This indifference is rooted in a confidence that God is in control and in a humility about our own ability to discern the workings of Providence in contemporary events. God often accomplishes his providential purposes in ways that we do not

---

[7]Ibid.
[8]Ibid., 343-44.

expect, so we should not be too quick to rejoice over what seems like a positive development or to despair over what seems like bad news. Further, as I'll discuss more later, we should be very cautious to claim that we can recognize what exactly God is doing in any given situation. For instance, Jeremiah declares the Babylonian king Nebuchadnezzar to be the "servant" of the Lord (Jer 43:10), and Isaiah calls King Cyrus of Persia the Lord's "anointed" (Is 45:1). Plainly, God can appoint pagan rulers to carry out his purposes, purposes that remain opaque and surprising to God's own people. As God declares to Isaiah in elaborating on how he will use Cyrus, "I form light and create darkness; / I make well-being and create calamity; / I am the LORD, who does all these things" (Is 45:7).

Of course the most obvious example of the unpredictable workings of Providence is the passion and death of Jesus. Jesus' own disciples certainly thought these events constituted unmitigated bad news, and yet "we call this Friday good."[9] As one of G. K. Chesterton's protagonists declares, "The cross cannot be defeated, . . . for it is Defeat."[10] Epistemic humility, particularly regarding the workings of Providence, requires us to acknowledge that even when our candidate loses, or when a court case is decided in a way that seems wrong, or when tragedy strikes, God is still working out his will—and he cannot be defeated. The reverse holds true as well: it may be that just when we think we are winning, we are going astray from God's kingdom. A high view of Providence and a chastened sense of our ability to recognize God's methods of victory frees us from worrying about whether a given event is good or bad. Even

[9]T. S. Eliot, "East Coker," in *Collected Poems, 1909–1962* (New York: Harcourt Brace Jovanovich, 1991), 188.
[10]G. K. Chesterton, "The Ball and the Cross," in *The Collected Works of G. K. Chesterton*, vol. 7, *The Ball and the Cross, Manalive, The Flying Inn*, intro. and notes by Iain T. Benson (San Francisco: Ignatius Press, 2004), 152.

when the events of the news seem irredeemably evil, they remain under the hand of the Creator who is working all things according to his plan.

The theologian Paul Griffiths draws two implications from Pascal's view of Providence and his recommendations regarding how we should engage in public controversies. The first is that we "should engage in controversy with a level of energy and commitment appropriate to the importance of the topic and to the degree of certitude [we] have about the truth of [our] preferred position on that topic."[11] We *should* be passionate about some issues, but our media environment tends to warp our emotional scales. We can get all worked up parsing some ambiguous tweet or imputing the worst possible motives to some public figure's off-the-cuff comments, and at the same time, we may be neglecting far more important and substantive—but less superficially exciting—developments related to climate change, systemic poverty, or the conditions of migrant workers in our home town. Perhaps we need to conduct an emotional audit and consider which issues or news items cause us to become angry, outraged, or excited: Are we grieving over what grieves God and rejoicing over what brings him joy? Or have we become emotionally invested in trivia while growing apathetic about matters of real import?

The second implication is that regardless of the issue and the appropriate level of passion with which we advocate it, we "should have no concern for the outcome."[12] As Pascal himself writes, "We act as if it were our mission to make truth triumph whilst it is only our mission to combat for it."[13] We should be passionate in

---

[11]Paul J. Griffiths, *Decreation: The Last Things of All Creatures* (Waco, TX: Baylor University Press, 2014), 345.
[12]Ibid.
[13]Pascal, *Blaise Pascal: Thoughts*, 344.

working for what we perceive to be the good, but we should not be upset if our cause faces setbacks or receives bad news.

It is important to be clear here regarding what Pascal is and is not recommending. Some might worry that his quietism is too passive, too culpably unconcerned with matters of real importance. Yet, as Griffiths clarifies, Pascal enjoins "quietism with respect to political interest, not with respect to politics *simpliciter*."[14] Indeed, the paradoxical truth may be that if we care less about whether our side is winning, we may be more able to bear faithful political witness: "Political advocacy would be more fruitful if interest in its outcome were quieted."[15] This is not some sort of Stoic resignation; Pascal invites us to care deeply about the issues to which God has called us but to care without worrying about the score, the outcome.

Such a stance is hard to maintain in our media environment because so many news stories are framed as a kind of contest, with clear winners and losers. The media's horse-race election coverage, breathless adjudicating of how some court decision will reshape the battle lines of the culture war, and endless parsing of the latest polls shape us to view every news story as a scoreboard update. When Donald Trump was running for president, he exploited this obsession. As he proclaimed at one campaign rally, "We're going to win so much, you may even get tired of winning. And you'll say, 'Please, please, it's too much winning, we can't take it anymore. Mr. President, it's too much.' And I'll say, 'No it isn't, we have to keep winning, we have to win more, we're going to win more.' We're going to win so much. . . . You will be so happy."[16] And yet as Pascal reminds us, Christian

---

[14]Griffiths, *Decreation*, 339.
[15]Ibid., 340.
[16]Donald Trump, "You Gonna Win So Much You May Even Get Tired of Winning," YouTube, May 20, 2016, www.youtube.com/watch?v=daOH-pTd_nk.

happiness does not depend on receiving news of some temporal victory. Indeed, an obsessive focus on the metrics of victory drains psychic energy, induces mental and emotional dyspepsia, and distracts us from the good work we can do. When we trust in Providence, we are freed from emotional overinvestment in the day's drama. Fixating on winning may be a good strategy for politicians and media companies, but it's not a Christian way of attending to the events of our day.

The goal of *sancta indifferentia* is faithful action that's not concerned with the results. Thoreau stands as a good example here: for all his talk about attending to "the mountain-brooks, the Parnassian streams," he involved himself personally in many social and political affairs.[17] Besides helping escaped slaves to freedom and going to jail over his refusal to pay taxes that would support an unjust war, his speech passionately defending John Brown after the failed Harpers Ferry raid changed the tide of public sentiment and galvanized support for abolition.[18] His essay "Civil Disobedience" inspired and informed subsequent generations of protestors, including Gandhi and Martin Luther King Jr. Thoreau's posture of indifference to trivial dramas enabled him to discern how he should respond to the more fundamental currents of his time. As Thoreau wrote to a friend shortly after the outbreak of the Civil War,

> The most fatal and indeed the only fatal, weapon you can direct against evil, ever [is to ignore it]; for as long as you *know* of it, you are *particeps criminis* [a partner in crime]. What business have you, if you are 'an angel of light,' to be pondering over the deeds of darkness, reading the New

---

[17]Henry David Thoreau, *Reform Papers*, ed. Wendell Glick, Writings of Henry David Thoreau (Princeton, NJ: Princeton University Press, 1973), 172.

[18]Laura Dassow Walls, *Henry David Thoreau: A Life* (Chicago: University of Chicago Press, 2017), 449-56.

York Herald, & the like? . . . Blessed were the days before
you read a president's message.[19]

Thoreau—like Pascal—knew that reveling in the day's political
news, news that he could do nothing about, would only distract
and disturb him without improving the situation in the slightest.
When we scroll through our news feed each morning to see if
our side of a particular issue is winning, we betray a lack of trust
in Providence. Of course this is not the only way to engage the
news. We can also rely on the news to form our judgment and
guide our actions in response to contingent political or social
matters. Such use of the news is entirely congruent with a Pascalian *sancta indifferentia.*

Before exploring further this kind of attention that enables
responsible action, I need to address a concern that may be
lingering in readers' minds: Is indifference regarding the
outcome of particular causes, the success or failure of our side,
simply the luxury of those safely ensconced in privileged, secure
positions? For instance, if one is an illegal immigrant, perhaps
one doesn't have the luxury of being indifferent to the political
fortunes of a bill regarding immigration. Or if one is a racial
minority, perhaps one doesn't have the luxury of being indifferent to the election of a racist police chief.

Certainly apathy can be an attitude of the privileged who are
insulated from the effects of bad news, but holy apathy is also
the attitude of the martyrs who faithfully obey God regardless
of the events swirling around them, events that they are powerless to control. In reality, we are all powerless to control the
outcome of the political, social, and cultural disputes of our
time, and the vast majority of us have little opportunity to

---

[19]Henry David Thoreau, *The Correspondence of Henry David Thoreau*, ed. Walter Harding and Carl Bode (New York: New York University Press, 1958), 611.

directly influence these battles; when we follow their developments with bated breath, rooting for our chosen side to win, we display a lack of faith in Providence and an outsized view of our own power. And the result is that we profane our minds, macadamizing them with trivial updates instead of meditating on eternal words so that we, like the blessed man of Psalm 1, can bear fruit to bless our neighbors in whatever situation we find ourselves.

Chagall is a helpful example here; as a Jew in 1930s Europe, he was certainly vulnerable to the noxious clouds of anti-Semitism. And indeed he barely escaped occupied France in 1941 on the infamously overcrowded SS *Navemar*. The attitude of the figure in *Solitude* is the attitude not of the privileged but of someone who knows he may become a martyr. Yet, regardless of the events sweeping through his city, the Jew in this painting prayerfully meditates on the beloved Scriptures. It is these words that he will strive to embody faithfully no matter the events of his time. Pascalian holy apathy is not the culpable indifference of the privileged, of those who can afford to wash their hands of contemporary affairs; it is the attitude embodied by the martyrs who commit to acting faithfully regardless of the consequences.

Thomas Merton's Contemplative Politics

Rightly oriented attention to the news, I have claimed, has two movements: an askesis that manifests as a *sancta indifferentia* regarding temporal dramas and a loving devotion to God and his word that leads to responsible action. Pascal helps us understand the need to turn away from the drama offered by the news-as-scoreboard, and the life and writings of the Trappist monk Thomas Merton can guide us as we consider how we should direct our attention. Merton lived as a hermit during the last few years of his life, but he remained deeply invested in the social issues of his day. While Merton doesn't couch his ideas in this manner, I think it's helpful to organize his thinking on the news as responding in turn to the three problems that Thoreau identified: an unhealthy fixation on the news can induce mental dyspepsia, make our intellects into passive thoroughfares, and misdirect our energies into hacking at the branches of evil. We'll consider these in reverse order.

Contemplation and complicity. As a contemplative monk, Merton devoted much of his time to practices that disciplined his attention. And by setting down the telescope proffered by the news media and turning his attention to his inner life, he turned also from the branches of evil—its distant and obvious symptoms—to its roots gripping his own soul. His writings turn again and again to his profound sense of complicity in the great evils of his day. One might think that a monk in Kentucky would have no responsibility for the rise of Nazism in Europe or the insidious rot of racism that the civil rights movement brought to light. But instead of casting blame on others, Merton sought to understand the ways in which he participated in these wrongs.

This awareness blossoms in an interior silence that requires a certain degree of exterior silence. Merton states flatly that "Christians should have quiet homes" and beware of the TV and radio with their incessant chatter: "Those who love God should attempt to preserve or create an atmosphere in which He can be found." The point of this askesis is an "interior silence," "but just as interior asceticism cannot be acquired without concrete and exterior mortification, so it is absurd to talk about interior silence where there is no exterior silence." Merton is not recommending that we ignore all that is going on in the world around us; rather, he's worried that we surround ourselves with noise in order to distract ourselves from those motives and desires at the ground of our being: "A world of propaganda, of endless argument, vituperation, criticism, or simply of chatter, is a world without anything to live for."[20] When we carve out space in which to be silent, we find ourselves confronted by what in fact we *are* living for. We may not be flattered by what we discover.

In the interior silence that contemplation opens, Merton recognizes his own complicity in the injustices of society. While the news-as-scoreboard model invites us to view ourselves as the "good guys" and blame our opponents for the ills of our culture, Merton insists that this binary view is simplistic and false. In actuality, as Alexander Solzhenitsyn famously wrote, "The line dividing good and evil cuts through the heart of every human being."[21] Merton takes the evil in his own heart with remarkable seriousness. One striking example is his claim that Hitler is a fruit of the social condemnation—the outrage culture, we might say today—that Merton participates in:

> When I pray for peace I pray for the following miracle. That God move all men to pray and do penance and recognize each one his own great guilt, because we are all guilty. . . . We are a tree, of which [Hitler] is one of the fruits, and we all nourish him, and he thrives most of all on our hatred and condemnation of him, when that condemnation disregards our own guilt, and piles the responsibility for everything upon somebody else's sins![22]

---

[20]Thomas Merton, *The Sign of Jonas* (New York: Harvest Books, 1981), 311-12.
[21]Alexandr Isaevich Solzhenitsyn, *The Gulag Archipelago 1918–1956: An Experiment in Literary Investigation, Parts I-II*, trans. Thomas P. Whitney (New York: Harper & Row, 1974), 168.
[22]Thomas Merton, *The Secular Journal of Thomas Merton* (New York: Farrar, Straus & Cudahy, 1959), 164-65.

How many of us who are outraged by one politician or another can recognize our impulse to condemn and hate as our complicity in the very sin we decry? Our political-entertainment industry generates what Neil Postman refers to as the "peek-a-boo" world of "Show Business."[23] Yet, instead of merely condemning this world, Merton's bracing prayer reminds us that insofar as we are entertained by this game of peek-a-boo, we are guilty.[24]

In *My Argument with the Gestapo*, Merton stages a dialogue that illuminates his efforts to face his own responsibility for the evils of his day. He imagines himself visiting England at the outbreak of World War II. At one point, Merton's fictionalized alter ego converses with another character about their responses to the Battle of Britain. She is confused because when she declares that "Germany is guilty," he replies, "I also am guilty for the war, partly." His Pascalian indifference to the outcome of the war is incomprehensible to her:

> "I stay up all night, I hang on to the walls and the explosions of bombs break my back in half, I live in black smoke of this city's burning, and the dust of the ruins is always in my throat. I don't want to know that nobody's responsible. I want to know that one man is. I haven't time to know anything less arbitrary than that. Tomorrow I may be dead."
>
> "What difference will it make, then, what political fact you happen to have known?"
>
> "I want to know who is responsible."
>
> "Even if it isn't really true?"

---

[23]Neil Postman, *Amusing Ourselves to Death: Public Discourse in the Age of Show Business* (New York: Penguin, 1986), 77, 63.

[24]I first developed portions of this section in an essay I wrote for the fiftieth anniversary of Merton's death. Jeffrey Bilbro, "Thomas Merton's Contemplative Politics," *Front Porch Republic*, December 10, 2018, www.frontporchrepublic .com/2018/12/thomas-mertons-contemplative-politics/.

"In the simple sense in which I want to know it, it will be true enough for me: I will have been killed by one of their bombers, and the symbol on the rudder will be enough for a judgment."

"You want to die, perfectly sure of who it is you hate?"

"Yes, why not? At least it is something definite to die with."

"Not definite enough for me, and not the kind of definiteness I want. I want to die knowing something besides double-talk."

"There is no such thing as double-talk, . . . not to me, there isn't. Not any more."

[They walk further in silence.]

"Is that what you are here to find out? Your part in what is happening? Do you want to know how much you yourself are responsible for?"

"You guessed it," I answered her.[25]

This conversation weaves together features of our contemporary political discourse—a sort of "post-truth" posture, an insistence on identifying (and destroying) villains, a desire for clear boundary lines delineating who is right and who is wrong. Yet Merton's contemplative politics resists these temptations by refusing to care about which side wins and by grounding action in a recognition of "how much you yourself are responsible for." Merton has confidence that God will carry out his will; hence, like Pascal, Merton's concern is with whether he himself is participating in this divine will. As he writes in a later book addressed to "a white liberal" regarding the civil rights movement, "Doubtless the mercy and truth of God, the victory of Christ, are being manifested in our current history, but I am not able to see

---

[25]Thomas Merton, *My Argument with the Gestapo* (New York: New Directions, 1975), 76-78.

how they are being manifested *by us*."[26] Thus, in his fictional
dialogue his questions finally lead his interlocutor to silence
and self-reflection. Instead of assigning blame to others, we
have to help one another reach the interior silence that will
allow us to recognize our own failings, our own responsibility
for injustice.

Merton's deep sense of complicity is shared by others who
learn to cultivate this interior silence. Thoreau realized that
paying taxes implicated him in the wars those taxes funded.
And Simone Weil likely harmed her own health by sharing the
rationed diet of those in occupied France; as her biographer
concludes, she "deprived herself because she didn't want to be
one of the privileged."[27] Such responses may seem extreme to
us, but those who turn away from the media's telescopic morality and cultivate interior stillness come to view the news not
as some spectacle to amuse us or as a scoreboard to tell us if our
side is winning. Instead, the news of what our neighbors are
going through invites us to enact our solidarity with them.

Antipoetry as resistance. Such contemplative attention
is difficult for several reasons. For one, humans fear interior
silence and seek out distractions. Further, as Merton points
out, we have developed technologies that are remarkably adept
at helping us maintain this state of distraction. But as his
mention of double-talk indicates, one of the chief barriers to
contemplative silence is the cacophony of slogans, hashtags,
and catch phrases with which we are bombarded. In their ab-
straction and absurdity, these phrases do violence to the world
in which we live. Hence, instead of allowing his mind to
become a passive thoroughfare for such trivial language,

---

[26]Thomas Merton, *Seeds of Destruction* (New York: Farrar, Straus and Giroux,
    1965), 27.
[27]Simone Pétrement, *Simone Weil: A Life* (New York: Pantheon Books, 1976), 517.

Merton developed a mode of antipoetry as one way of resisting the incursions of double-talk. Merton defines *antipoetry* as "a deliberate ironic feedback of cliché."[28] By taking an advertising slogan or a politician's slick claim and reworking it in a poem, antipoetry aims to break the spell of this language and cause the reader to question its meaning. In effect, an antipoem invites us to ruminate, *hagah*, on the ephemeral language that surrounds us in order to realize how vapid it is. Clichés cannot sustain rumination; the more one chews on them, the less they mean. This exercise saps such language of its hypnotic power. The self-serious proclamations of world leaders, the chattering of the coastal class, the declamations of the extreme online—all these lose their magic spell when transformed into antipoetry.

Perhaps it is helpful to compare Merton's antipoetry to a modern technological innovation: active noise-canceling headphones. These headphones listen to ambient noise and broadcast it to the listener in the opposite polarity, resulting in destructive interference and near silence. Antipoetry listens to the linguistic static of the culture and feeds it back in the opposite polarity— from art and not from a place of power—resulting in words that are out of phase and induce silence.[29]

For instance, in one poem, "Epitaph for a Public Servant," Merton recycles the absurd statements that Adolf Eichmann, a Nazi official who oversaw the transport of Jews to concentration camps, made during his trial, statements such as, "'Not out of mercy / Did I launch this transaction.'"[30] In another

---

[28]Thomas Merton, *The Asian Journal of Thomas Merton*, rev. ed., ed. Patrick Hart et al. (New York: New Directions, 1975), 286.
[29]This analogy and portions of the analysis that follow are drawn from my scholarly essay on Merton's antipoetry. Jeffrey Bilbro, "From Violence to Silence: The Rhetorical Means and Ends of Thomas Merton's Antipoetry," *Merton Annual: Studies in Culture, Spirituality and Social Concerns* 22 (2009): 120-39.
[30]Thomas Merton, "48," in *The Collected Poems of Thomas Merton* (New York: New Directions, 1980), 703.

poem, subtitled "(NEWSCAST)," Merton scrambles news-
speak into unpunctuated nonsense:

> All important Washington dolls
> Continue today the burning of forbidden customs
> Printed joys are rapidly un-deciphered
> As from the final page remain
> No more than the perfumes
> And military shadows
> President says the affair must now warn
> All the star-secret homespuns and undecided face-makers[31]

Merton would similarly have eviscerated the hashtags and trite
bromides that compose so much of our discourse today: a series
of Trump tweets or the techno-utopian pronouncements of Elon
Musk would provide rich fodder for Merton's poetic imagination.
The result of his ironic feedback of such language is a resounding
silence. As Patrick O'Connell explains of Merton's antipoetry,

> By pushing the abuse of language to the point of absurdity,
> by exposing, not just parodying, the meaningless babble
> of contemporary discourse, the poet has cleared the way
> for a movement into the silence and emptiness of contem-
> plation. . . . "Anti-poetry" can function as a *via negativa*
> that impels one to silence by inducing revulsion from its
> meaningless cacophony.[32]

We must first cleanse our minds of self-serving political and advertising slogans before we can enter into a clear-minded silence.
    Merton's antipoetry cultivates a resistance to the violent and
irresponsible language whose cacophony threatens to destroy

---

[31]Ibid., 427.
[32]Patrick F. O'Connell, *Cables to the Ace, or Familiar Liturgies of Misunderstanding*, in *The Thomas Merton Encyclopedia*, ed. William H. Shannon,
Christine M. Bochen, and Patrick F. O'Connell (Maryknoll, NY: Orbis Books,
2002), 38.

our ability to converse and think with one another. If we are not careful, such language turns our minds into macadamized thoroughfares for the clichés of money and power and entertainment. This self-justifying language of power "can quickly contaminate the thinking of everybody," in large part because such language is unable to acknowledge our complicity in injustice or wrong.[33] But if, following Pascal, we are indifferent to power—to winning—the temptations of such self-justifying language will have no hold on us. Paradoxically, then, ruminating in a poetic register on the vapid clichés that fill our social media feeds can lead us to an interior silence. And this silence forms the space we need to think more deeply about the issues facing us and our neighbors so that we may discern how to respond in love.

The hour of vocation. As Thoreau warned, flitting from one news tidbit to the next induces mental dyspepsia, and yet Merton does not recommend simply abstaining from the news. In fact, he explicitly warns that we must avoid a "secession into individualistic concern with one's own salvation alone" as this "may in fact leave the way all the more open for unscrupulous men and groups to gain and wield unjust power."[34] Instead of a turning away from the world, his contemplative silence creates the interior space necessary to discern the particular issues to which we may be called to attend and respond. This silence is essential to maintaining our freedom to hear God's call and participate in his redemptive work. Merton puts it this way in the bracing preface to *Seeds of Destruction*:

> I hold that the contemplative life of the Christian is not a life of abstraction, of secession, in order to concentrate upon ideal essences, upon absolutes, upon eternity alone.

---

[33]Thomas Merton, *Thomas Merton on Peace* (New York: McCall, 1971), 241.
[34]Merton, *Seeds of Destruction*, 112.

Christianity cannot reject history. It cannot be a denial of time. Christianity is centered on an historical event which has changed the meaning of history. The freedom of the Christian contemplative is not freedom *from* time, but freedom *in* time. It is the freedom to go out and meet God in the inscrutable mystery of His will here and now, in this precise moment in which He asks man's cooperation in shaping the course of history according to the demands of divine truth, mercy and fidelity.[35]

Merton's approach to the news, then, entails focused attention to particular topics. We can't—indeed, we shouldn't— be informed about everything. But to what issues might God be calling us to attend? Our aim, as Merton puts it, should be to "listen to the voice of God in the events of the time" and faithfully obey.[36]

In Merton's case, his efforts to listen to the voice of God led him toward issues such as racial injustice, nuclear proliferation, and interreligious dialogue. In the mid-1960s, Merton wrote regarding the civil rights struggle that

this most critical moment in American history is . . . the hour of vocation, the moment in which, hearing and understanding the will of God as expressed in the urgent need of our Negro brother, we can respond to that inscrutable will in a faith that faces the need of reform and creative change, in order that the demands of truth and justice may not go unfulfilled.[37]

In making this claim, Merton was following his own advice to read history as a record of God's work in his world:

---

[35]Ibid., xiv.
[36]Ibid., 89.
[37]Ibid., 65.

The mystery of Christ is at work in all human events, and our comprehension of secular events works itself out and expresses itself in that sacred history, the history of salvation, which the Holy Spirit teaches us to perceive in events that appear to be purely secular. We have to admit that this meaning is often provisional and sometimes beyond our grasp. Yet as Christians, we are committed to an attempt to read an ultimate and transcendent meaning in temporal events that flow from human choices.[38]

The problem is that our human tendency is to read the news by the light of idolatrous standards, to ask not "Where might God's hand be in these events?" but "How will this affect my pocketbook?"[39] or "Is this spectacle entertaining?" or "Does this mean my side of some cultural or political battle is winning?"

To more consistently read the news by the divine light, we must learn to put down these false standards. To return to the *sancta indifferentia* with which we began this chapter, those who relinquish their desire to win some political or cultural contest will be more likely to perceive God's redemptive hand in the events of the day. Merton points to several exemplars in this regard: the civil rights marchers' courage, he claims, stemmed from their firm belief "that the victory of truth is inevitable," even if they might suffer for standing up for this truth.[40] Similarly, for Mahatma Gandhi "political action . . . was not a means to acquire security and strength for one's self and one's party, but a means of witnessing to the truth and the reality of the cosmic structure by making one's own proper contribution to the order willed by God. One could thus preserve one's integrity and peace, being detached from results

---

[38]Ibid., 112.
[39]Ibid., 23.
[40]Ibid., 44.

(which are in the hand of God)."[41] When we leave the outcome in God's hands, we receive the courage to do what is right regardless of the consequences. A contemplative response to the news, then, depends on eschatological hope, on fixing one's identity in a victory that lies outside the vicissitudes of daily news and politics.

In part two, on time, I'll consider more fully how we might read the news in the context of this eschatological horizon, but for now I trust it has become clear how, for Merton, pursuing a contemplative life and pursuing temporal justice are inseparable. As Henri Nouwen noted, "The great power of Merton as a writer still remains in his ability to comment on the concrete happenings of the day, and to do this out of a contemplative silence."[42] If more Christians would approach the news from this place of contemplative silence, of deeply rooted faith in God's redemptive work and eventual victory, the church's witness would shine more brightly amid the chaotic noise of the daily news. As Chagall's meditative figure reminds us, Christians should be wary of being caught up in the trivia of the day and should be devoted to eternal truths. This is the posture of the martyrs—faithful to the Word, indifferent to victory.

In a letter written on New Year's Day 1962, reflecting on the intractable problems raised by the proliferation of nuclear weapons, Merton quotes the "mighty theologian" Julian of Norwich: "Though 'all manner of things shall be well,' we cannot help but be aware, on the threshold of 1962 that we have enormous responsibilities and tasks of which we are perhaps no longer capable." The letter concludes, "I wanted to say these few things, as we enter the New Year. For it is going to be a

---

[41]Ibid., 227.
[42]Henri J. M. Nouwen, *Thomas Merton: Contemplative Critic* (San Francisco: Harper & Row, 1981), 39.

crucial year, and in it we are going to have to walk sanely, and in faith, and with great sacrifice, and with an almost impossible hope."[43] Merton, like Pascal, did not suffer from a macadamized mind. He was able to walk in hope through times of great turmoil because his habits of attention had rooted him deeply in the Word of God.

To TRUST IN God IS WHAT WE SHOULD DO. NOT TO FIGHT FOR SOME KIND OF VICTORY ON CONTROVERSIAL ISSUES, JUST TO PROVE THAT WE'RE CORRECT IN OUR OPINIONS & PERSPECTIVES. GoD ALLOWS SOME PEOPLE TO HAVE RIGHT PERSPECTIVE & HE ALSO ALLOWS THE OPPOSITE. NO MATTER THE RESULTS GoD'S PLAN WILL ALWAYS BE CARRIED OUT.

REBECCA

[43]Merton, *Seeds of Destruction*, 265.

Chapter Three

Liturgies of Attention

EACH OF THIS BOOK'S three parts concludes with some suggestions for how we might practice redemptive modes of reading the news. Christians have long been concerned not only with orthodoxy but also with orthopraxy. In recent years, Jamie Smith's excellent Cultural Liturgies series has reinvigorated this concern and brought renewed focus to the daily habits or liturgies that shape our theology.[1] As Tish Harrison Warren reminds us, important theological truths must be "borne out—lived, believed, and enfleshed—in the small moments of our day, in the places, seasons, homes, and communities that compose our lives."[2] In the context of the news, good intentions to root ourselves in God's Word and cultivate wise habits of attention won't count for much if the TV is constantly running in the background of our homes or if the first activity of our day is scrolling through a social media feed.

Read the Eternities

Thoreau challenges us to "Read not the Times. Read the Eternities."[3] If this was wise advice in the mid-nineteenth century,

---

[1]The first book in this series is the best place to start: James K. A. Smith, *Desiring the Kingdom: Worship, Worldview, and Cultural Formation*, Cultural Liturgies 1 (Grand Rapids, MI: Baker Academic, 2009).

[2]Tish Harrison Warren, *Liturgy of the Ordinary: Sacred Practices in Everyday Life* (Downers Grove, IL: InterVarsity Press, 2016), 23.

[3]Henry David Thoreau, *Reform Papers*, ed. Wendell Glick, Writings of Henry David Thoreau (Princeton, NJ: Princeton University Press, 1973), 173.

it's even more important for those of us who inhabit a digital media ecosystem. One way to understand the stakes is to put Thoreau's advice in terms of his dietetic metaphor: we should avoid marshmallows and eat vegetables. Hot takes and clickbait, TV news broadcasts (which are often basically just comedy shows), and the one-liners that populate social media feeds are easy to consume, but they leave us bloated. If we want to attend to the needs of our neighbors, we'll need a more robust diet of thoughtful journalism, long-form essays, and books.

There's really no good reason to get your news from TV; doing so is more likely to turn you into a macadamized spectator than it is to equip you to be a healthy participant in the public sphere. Even TED talks are just highbrow forms of intellectual candy—macarons, say, to broadcast TV's tootsie rolls. These media privilege entertainment rather than contemplation. Isn't there a place for amusement and relaxation, you might ask? Sure, but so much of what people do under the rubric of unwinding or self-care doesn't actually re-create or restore; it scratches the itch of our restless souls and, by so doing, keeps the wounds from healing. What we may need is simply silence, long walks, or even the quiet work of washing the dishes by hand. Netflix isn't the balm of Gilead.

The good news is that if our tastes have been malformed, if we have a craving for the salts and fats of junk-food news, we can begin to change our cravings by changing what we consume. As John Sommerville puts it, "Right now your brain is like a sieve with the news pouring through. Start reading something substantial, and you'll lose all interest in watching journalists write in the sand."[4] Most people who have stopped drinking soda or given up other junk food can attest that in a few weeks

---

[4]C. John Sommerville, *How the News Makes Us Dumb: The Death of Wisdom in an Information Society* (Downers Grove, IL: InterVarsity Press, 2009), 151.

or months their cravings for these foods go away. Our tastes are trainable. Thus it is that the injunction to read books shouldn't be seen as some dreary moralistic advice to eat your peas and carrots. Rather, we should see Thoreau's advice as analogous to one of those cookbooks with lots of appealing pictures of home-cooked meals: their aim is to make us realize that fresh vegetables can actually taste *better* than junk food.

This is one of Alan Jacobs's points in his delightful *The Pleasures of Reading in an Age of Distraction*. Rather than telling people that they should read books because they are good for you, Jacobs says to "read at whim," to read the books that delight us.[5] Yet Jacobs is careful to distinguish between "*whim* and *Whim*. In its lower-case version, whim is thoughtless, directionless preference that almost invariably leads to boredom or frustration or both. But Whim is something very different."[6] Jacobs points to Auden's poetic description of vocation to identify the kind of rapt attention to which such Whim leads us:

> You need not see what someone is doing
> to know if it is his vocation,
>
> you have only to watch his eyes:
> a cook mixing a sauce, a surgeon
>
> making a primary incision,
> a clerk completing a bill of lading,
>
> wear that same rapt expression,
> forgetting themselves in a function.

---

[5] Alan Jacobs, *The Pleasures of Reading in an Age of Distraction* (New York: Oxford University Press, 2011), 15.

[6] Ibid., 41. Jacobs develops this distinction at length, and I'm simplifying his argument somewhat. He also seems to think that we can learn to follow Whim on our own even though his primary example in this regard is the historian Edward Gibbon, who only learned to follow Whim under the benevolent guidance of a personal tutor.

How beautiful it is,
that eye-on-the-object look.[7]

Those who follow Whim discover that in denying the lures of "the appetitive goddesses,"[8] they can enjoy the deep satisfactions of good work and good reading.

Perhaps the best way to begin retraining our tastes is to identify the contemporary topics that attract our attention, those that, as Merton writes, announce our "hour of vocation," and then go in search of older books that will deepen our understanding of these topics. C. S. Lewis, a fierce opponent of what he termed "presentism," suggests a simple guideline regarding our literary diet:

> It is a good rule, after reading a new book, never to allow yourself another new one till you have read an old one in between. If that is too much for you, you should at least read one old one to every three new ones. . . . Not, of course, that there is any magic about the past. People were no cleverer then than they are now; they made as many mistakes as we. But not the *same* mistakes.[9]

Lewis's advice is good as it stands. But in our day of information abundance, we could supplement it by saying that we ought to spend at least one—and probably more like two or three—minutes reading books or meaty essays for every minute we spend scrolling through a news feed, listening to the radio, or surfing around the internet checking in on the latest news. These

---

[7]W. H. Auden, "Sext," *Collected Poems*, repr. ed. (New York: Vintage, 1991), 629-30.

[8]Ibid.

[9]C. S. Lewis, "On the Reading of Old Books," in *God in the Dock: Essays on Theology and Ethics* (Grand Rapids, MI: Eerdmans, 1970), 201-2. For a wise consideration of how and why we should read old books, see Alan Jacobs, *Breaking Bread with the Dead: A Reader's Guide to a More Tranquil Mind* (New York: Penguin, 2020).

longer essays and older books act as a kind of ballast, helping us better discern which new headlines are actually significant.

Of course we can't read books about all the important issues of our day, but we aren't called to be experts about everything. What particular issues might God be calling you to? For Merton, nuclear weapons and racism were two issues he wrestled with intensely; he didn't speak to every issue of his day. So if we consider what particular topics God, through circumstances or promptings, might be calling us to study, we'll have a guide to what books or essays we should read. Perhaps you notice stories about racial injustice so you turn to books on the history of race in America, or you keep seeing news about climate change so you look for books to deepen your understanding of this complex phenomenon. As we become formed by such deep reading, we will be less prone to view the news as a scoreboard or a spectacle and better able to consider how God might be calling us to be faithfully present to our neighbors.

I am an academic—I read and write books for a living!—so following this practice should be easy for me, yet I constantly have to fight the temptation to read cotton candy rather than broccoli. The only way I manage to discipline my reading appetite, at least somewhat, is by putting boundaries in place. Following Andy Crouch's advice in *Tech-Wise Family*, I take several hours away from my computer each day, at least much of the day on Sunday, and a week or two off the internet each summer.[10] Probably more importantly, I don't own a smartphone, which is less of an inconvenience than many people assume and is a great help in avoiding distractions. Such boundaries provide the space I need away from the brouhaha of the moment so that I can more attentively read

---

[10]Andy Crouch, *The Tech-Wise Family: Everyday Steps for Putting Technology in Its Proper Place* (Grand Rapids, MI: Baker Books, 2017).

and contemplate lasting truths and then respond to current events with the fruits of this rumination.

Learn a Craft

Auden's poetic description of the attention required to pursue a vocation also relates to my second recommendation, which is to learn a craft. Writers from Kathleen Norris to Alex Langlands have demonstrated the power of mundane work, the ongoing work of care for people and objects in all their intractable materiality, to shape our souls.[11] When we grapple with physical reality, we become responsible—able to respond—to the needs of those around us. Cooking meals, building wooden furniture, or growing a garden may not seem relevant to how we consume the news, but such activities train us to attend to the world in restorative, redemptive ways.

[margin handwriting: DAILY CHORE MAY SEEM INSIGNIFICANT]

I mentioned earlier that Josef Pieper suggests that those who have lost the power to see clearly should abstain from "the visual noise of daily inanities at a distance." And he goes on to offer a "better and more immediately effective remedy . . . : *to be active oneself in artistic creation, producing shapes and forms for the eye to see.*" Artistic or artisanal work requires close attention: "The mere attempt, therefore, to create an artistic form compels the artist to take a fresh look at the visible reality; it requires authentic and personal observation."[12] Hence, artistic making trains us to relate to the world as those who tend and create rather than those who spectate and

---

[11]Alexander Langlands, *Cræft: An Inquiry into the Origins and True Meaning of Traditional Crafts* (New York: Norton, 2019); Kathleen Norris, *The Quotidian Mysteries: Laundry, Liturgy and "Women's Work"* (New York: Paulist Press, 1998). See also Matthew B. Crawford, *The World Beyond Your Head: On Becoming an Individual in an Age of Distraction* (New York: Farrar, Straus & Giroux, 2015).

[12]Josef Pieper, *Only the Lover Sings: Art and Contemplation*, trans. Lothar Krauth (San Francisco: Ignatius Press, 1990), 35.

consume. Indeed, in a profound way the loving attention of a human maker parallels the Creator's love for creation.

Pieper focuses on the way that "fine" arts—activities like music, painting, or poetry—train our attention, but even the more mundane work of cooking or carpentry, sewing or gardening, doing the laundry or washing the dishes, forces us to engage with particular, material realities. In doing so, we learn to respond to the limitations and needs of our material: a cook adds flour until a roux gains the right thickness; a carpenter follows the grain of the wood; a gardener props up a weak tomato plant. One of the great celebrants of this quotidian work of care is Kathleen Norris. She acknowledges that such work has often been relegated to women or to members of particular races or classes. As she puts it, "Cleaning up after others, or even ourselves, is not what we educate our children to do; it's for someone else's children, the less intelligent, less educated and less well-off."[13] And yet she finds that ordinary activities like "walking, baking bread and doing laundry" help her develop a posture of "contemplation."[14] Moreover, for Norris, the fine arts and these quotidian arts are profoundly analogous: writing a "poem, like housekeeping itself, is an attempt to bring order out of chaos."[15] In seeking to cultivate a craft, we don't have to start by taking piano lessons, although that would be good! We can begin now with the humble work of daily living. As the philosopher Albert Borgmann notes, even "inconspicuous, homely" activities like "music, gardening, the culture of the table, or running" can become "focal . . . practices" that reinvigorate our relation to the physical world.[16]

---

[13]Norris, *Quotidian Mysteries*, 5.
[14]Ibid., 15.
[15]Ibid., 34.
[16]Albert Borgmann, *Technology and the Character of Contemporary Life: A Philosophical Inquiry* (Chicago: University of Chicago Press, 1987), 197.

Similarly, in his book on the repertoire of crafts by which peasants in England made their livelihoods and cared for their places, Alexander Langlands develops Richard Sennett's claim that "craftsmanship [is] the state of being engaged."[17] Langlands suggests that the recent spate of "craft-oriented writing" stems from our sense that we are disconnected from the world: "We have become detached from making, and it isn't a good state for us to be in. It's unhealthy when we are disconnected from making."[18] When we rely on the skill of other people—or, increasingly, machines—we become detached from the world. Learning the skilled arts of care connects us redemptively to our homes. It leads to the particular, tactile contemplation of the craftsperson: attending with one's whole body to the materials at hand, working with their particular properties to make something beautiful and useful.[19]

This recommendation to learn a craft might seem rather disconnected from learning to attend well to the news. Yet Simone Weil talks about how doing math homework—even if you're bad at math; in fact, especially if you're bad at math—can cultivate the kind of sustained attention necessary for prayer.[20] Cultivating a craft can have a similar effect. Even if our efforts are bumbling, we'll be learning how to attend to and care for a portion of the world. Such work reminds us that part of our call as humans, part of what it means to be made in the image of God, is to care for creation. In cultivating a craft, then, we can be doing good, responsible work while at the same time forming our souls to attend in ways that befit our call to tend and keep creation.

[17]Langlands, *Cræft*, 11.
[18]Ibid., 337.
[19]Ibid., 342.
[20]Simone Weil, *Waiting for God*, trans. Emma Craufurd (New York: Harper & Row, 1973), 106-7, 109.

If our souls have become warped by attending to distant spectacles or by obsessing about the outcome of dramas over which we have no control, the discipline of learning a craft can be a vital antidote. Perhaps the news to which we most need to attend won't be found on social media feeds or the front page of any paper. Instead, it's the cry of a baby who needs her diaper changed. It's the bubbles bursting from a pot that needs to be stirred. It's the ripple of wood grain we have to accommodate in shaping a handle. These are the news alerts, the "push notifications," to which we can respond with skill. And such work inculcates a properly responsible attention, an attention that seeks to lovingly care for the needs at hand.

WE SHOULD ATTEND TO THE PEOPLE AND EVENTS AROUND US. NOT ON NEWSPAPER HEADLINES. WE MUST TRY TO GET RID OF OUR APPETITE FOR 'EASY FOOD'.

REBECCA

PART 2

Time

Chapter Four

Kairos Versus Chronos

WHAT TIME IS IT? This may seem like a simple question, but there are many ways to answer it: my phone tells me it's 6:18 a.m.; the calendar tells me it's May 25; my prayer book tells me it's the thirty-fifth day of Easter; the sun tells me it's just past sunrise, and my brain tells me it's time for another cup of coffee. The differences between these answers may seem trivial, but the standard by which we tell time determines to a profound extent what events we see as significant or newsworthy. Indeed, one of the reasons our culture has an unhealthy obsession with the news is because its sense of time is off kilter. If we want to learn how to read the news Christianly, we'll have to learn to tell time Christianly. *[handwritten: CHRISTIAN STANDARD OF TIME. BINGO!]*

We can distinguish between two broad understandings of time by way of the Greek words *kairos* and *chronos*. *Kairos* refers to the propitious time, time that is right for a certain act—the time to plant or harvest a crop, for instance. *Kairos* time is rhythmic, cyclical, seasonal. *Chronos*, as its English derivative *chronological* indicates, is closer to our modern understanding of time. This is time as quantifiable duration, as something that is linear and sequential. Insofar as the news is, by definition, concerned with what is happening "now," it is rooted in chronos.

Theologian Paul Griffiths elaborates on this basic distinction through another pair of terms: *systolic* and *metronomic*. *Metronomic* is fairly clear as a description of chronos, and he gets

[handwritten: MODERN UNDERSTANDING OF TIME. LIKE 5 O'CLOCK.]

the term *systolic* from 1 Corinthians 7, where Paul discusses how Christians should think about marriage now that "time has grown very short"; in Greek the phrase is *kairos systellō* (1 Cor 7:29). This passage has often been read as indicating Paul's expectation of Christ's imminent return, but the Greek refers to time being bunched or folded; it is *systolated*, which Griffiths translates expansively as "ruched, pleated, tensed, furled, crouched like a cat for the spring, tight-wrapped in grave-clothes like a corpse prepared for resurrection, swaddled like a newborn being carried toward the baptismal font."[1] It's not that Paul is warning that metronomic time is about to run out; rather, he's naming how the person of Christ should reorder our conception of time: "The crucifixion, resurrection, and ascension of Jesus lie at the heart of time. . . . Time is contracted by these events, pleated and folded around them, gathered by them into a tensely dense possibility."[2]

Yet while time is fundamentally systolated around the person of Christ, metronomic time remains a feature of our fallen creaturely life as well, and Christians have to learn how to live within both these modes of time. Griffiths speculates that in heaven redeemed creation will exist not in some static, undifferentiated eternity but in one that is rhythmic, patterned by the triune life. In the interim, however, we are present in both the metronomic ticking of chronos and the systolated pattern of kairos. And these two types of time provide contrasting horizons of meaning against which we must learn to judge events and recognize their proper proportion and significance.

Griffiths's way of framing our temporal dilemma is particularly Christian, but the tension between kairos and chronos is

---

[1] Paul J. Griffiths, *Decreation: The Last Things of All Creatures* (Waco, TX: Baylor University Press, 2014), 95-96.
[2] Ibid., 96.

more fundamentally human. After all, the language of the New Testament is working with a distinction that already exists in the Greek language, and in the remainder of this chapter I'll consider other ways humans have responded to it. In general, some cultures overemphasize kairos and others, such as our contemporary Western culture, overemphasize chronos. This matters crucially because the way we tell time provides the standard by which we judge an event's significance, its newsworthiness. TIME STANDARD : JUDGE NEWSWORTHINESS

As we'll discover, we wouldn't care so much about the news if our culture weren't shaped by a deep, fundamental belief in progress. For most of human history, people assumed that
OF TIME
empires and societies rose, prospered, and fell but that, as a whole, human civilization was neither improving nor declining. Beginning in the eighteenth century, however, a belief in progress took root, and this belief continues to color the background of our cultural consciousness, particularly in America. Such a belief, as we will see, leads to an overemphasis on current events and encourages observers to ascribe meaning to them using a historical frame rather than a figural one. As Christians, however, we should not ask whether an individual or occurrence is on the "right side of history"; instead, we should seek to discern how the events of our day might participate in the drama of God's ongoing redemption of creation.

Keeping Time and Interpreting the News

Perhaps the most incisive book about how different ways of telling time affect different cultural representations of reality—and hence different ways of interpreting the news—is Erich Auerbach's 1946 *Mimesis*. This may seem like an odd work to draw from to help us think about the news, but *Mimesis* will be our

touchstone through much of this part on time.[3] A brief introduction to Auerbach's life and work may elucidate why I think he
is an essential guide to making sense of how the news media report
events. Auerbach was a German Jew who earned his doctorate in
law before the outbreak of World War I. He spent four years
fighting in the German army, and after the war he shifted from law
to literature and earned a doctorate in Romance philology. He was
carving out a career for himself and publishing on Dante and Vico,
but in 1935 Nazi racial laws forced him from his professorship at
a German university, and he moved to Istanbul, where he taught
and wrote until the conclusion of World War II. It was while he
was living in exile, watching his nation wreak destruction on his
fellow Jews and so many others, that he wrote *Mimesis*.[4]

Auerbach certainly lived through many newsworthy events, yet
as a Jew he found himself on the wrong side of the Nazi version of
history, and this experience seems to have led him to investigate
other ways of judging the meaning of his life and its historical
context. So, although *Mimesis* is a scholarly book that proceeds
through close readings and careful analysis, it is also, as Edward
Said explains, "a personal book."[5] When confronted with the arc
of Nazi historical ideology, an arc that bends toward the glorious
supremacy of the Aryan "master race," Auerbach sought an alternative way to ascribe significance to individuals and events.

Auerbach frames his narrative as a historical survey of how
literary authors represent everyday life. In brief, he argues that

---

[3]Interestingly, Auerbach also wrote an essay on Pascal's political theory, and he
draws heavily on the letter I highlighted in chap. 2. Erich Auerbach, "On the
Political Theory of Pascal," in *Scenes from the Drama of European Literature*,
Theory and History of Literature 9 (Minneapolis: University of Minnesota
Press, 1984), 101-29.

[4]Jan N. Bremmer, "Erich Auerbach and His Mimesis," *Poetics Today* 20, no. 1
(1999): 4-6; and Edward W. Said, introduction to *Mimesis: The Representation
of Reality in Western Literature,* by Erich Auerbach, 50th anniv. ed. (Princeton, NJ: Princeton University Press, 2013), ix-xxxii.

[5]Said, introduction, xvii.

Homer and other authors of classic antiquity maintained a separation of styles: a high, serious, and sometimes tragic style was used to portray the activities of nobility or gods, and a low, comic style was used for the vulgar affairs of everyone else. The incarnation of Christ violated this division, and the spread of Christianity led to different ways of interweaving the high and the low, of ascribing significance to everyday occurrences. The two most prominent forms of realistic mingling were (1) the Christian figural realism that developed in the twelfth century and (2) the historical realism that developed in revolutionary France and came to dominate modernity.

To put it crudely, we can group the ways that cultures represent "contemporary everyday social reality," what we might simply call the news, into three categories.[6] Cultures that keep time according to kairos cycles fall into the first category: these view human civilization as relatively static and downplay the lasting significance of contemporary events. Cultures that follow chronos time fall into the second category: human civilization is progressing, and we can chart this progress in current affairs. Communities in the third category, which is the subject of the next chapter, seek to fit today's news into a kairos drama: Christians believe the events of time have been caught up into the life and redemptive work of Christ. This way of framing matters oversimplifies Auerbach's nuanced narrative, but it provides a serviceable heuristic to guide readers through the discussion that follows.

Overvaluing Kairos

All the newspapers and TV reports and online essays published today will carry the same date, regardless of where they originate.

---

[6]Auerbach, *Mimesis*, 518.

This is a remarkable feat of global synchronicity that would be unimaginable for most of human history. Those of us who take this homogeneous calendar for granted can have a hard time grasping what it would be like to live within a local, idiosyncratic dating system. Such systems were keyed to various kairos cycles, and societies that relied on them perceived history in essentially static terms. Fortune's wheel may move different individuals up and down, but there is no "arc" of history, no possibility of news that would fundamentally disrupt life's endless cycles.

Before the adoption of an absolute timescale, societies used local events to mark time. For instance, people might describe something by reference to the year that a great flood or earthquake occurred. The Greeks sometimes marked years by the winner of the Olympiad.[7] And many cultures used variants of a regnal system, in which events are pegged to the ruler under which they occurred. This made identifying particular years awkward, to say the least. When Luke wants to explain when John the Baptist began to preach, he correlates the year with the reigns of seven different people: "In the fifteenth year of the reign of Tiberius Caesar, Pontius Pilate being governor of Judea, and Herod being tetrarch of Galilee, and his brother Philip tetrarch of the region of Ituraea and Trachonitis, and Lysanias tetrarch of Abilene, during the high priesthood of Annas and Caiaphas, the word of God came to John the son of Zechariah in the wilderness" (Lk 3:1-2). These kinds of regnal calendars restart every time a new king comes to power; time starts over every generation. Thus they mark a mode of kairos, cyclic time.

Ironically, our modern system of dating was developed by a monk who was calculating Easter tables (a way for churches to

[7]Bonnie J. Blackburn and Leofranc Holford-Strevens, *The Oxford Companion to the Year: An Exploration of Calendar Customs and Time-Reckoning* (Oxford: Oxford University Press, 1999), 769.

determine when to celebrate Easter). Dionysius Exiguus counted the years from Christ's incarnation to avoid using the regnal years of Emperor Diocletian, who was a vicious persecutor of Christians.[8] The Venerable Bede's eighth-century *Ecclesiastical History of the English People* popularized this timeline and extrapolated it to refer to dates before Christ as well. This absolute, homogeneous system—one that has now been adopted around the globe—invites us to experience time in a linear fashion. It opens space for a kind of historical consciousness that seems to have been foreign to people who relied on cyclical, local methods of dating.

In describing the histories composed by classical authors like Petronius and Tacitus, who wrote in the first and second centuries AD, Auerbach notes that they paid attention to "neither social history nor economic history nor cultural history."[9] And this lack of historical consciousness coincides with an inability to give the events of their times—the news, as it were—historical or moral weight.[10] Such cultures didn't develop the sense of history that we take for granted; the time that matters to them isn't a chronological, linear time but a kairos, cyclic time.

A culture that runs on kairos predominantly values the actions of the royalty or the priestly class. Members of these groups carry out the cultic rituals that ensure divine favor and the normal cycles of the earth. The behavior of the kings determines whether the gods will bless their rule, and the priests'

---

[8]Ibid., 778-81. Paul Kosmin points to the Seleucid Era, which is named after a successor to Alexander the Great and counts up from 311 BC, as the first comprehensive and consistent dating system, the progenitor of our modern *anno Domini* method. Paul J. Kosmin, *Time and Its Adversaries in the Seleucid Empire* (Cambridge, MA: Belknap Press of Harvard University Press, 2018). See also Georges Declercq, *Anno Domini: The Origins of the Christian Era* (Turnhout, Belgium: Brepols, 2000).

[9]Auerbach, *Mimesis*, 40.

[10]Ibid., 33.

regular sacrifices bring about the rain and sun needed to produce abundant crops. Think, for instance, of the many classical myths—like Persephone and Hades, or Osiris and Isis— that explain the natural seasons, or the Buddhist bhavachakra symbol, the wheel of life that conveys a similar understanding of time as endless cycles. In such cultures, the news has little significance because there is no progress, no arc of history, just an endless recurrence that is punctuated by cultic acts.

[margin note: REPETITION OF DAILY RITUALS, NOTHING ELSE.]

A corollary of this bifurcation between those who participate in the divine, kairos cycles and those who do not is a fairly strict separation of literary styles: a high, serious style represents matters relating to the nobility, and a low, comic style deals with mundane matters. As Auerbach puts it, such cultures develop "a hierarchy of forms of expression [that] corresponds to a hierarchy of topics."[11] The lives of the elites have importance because they can participate in the cyclic divine order—indeed, in some cultures these classes were actually thought to be descended from the gods—but hoi polloi have no meaningful role to play in this drama. Hence, the events of their lives don't merit serious consideration.

[margin note: THINK TOO LOWLY OF INSIGNIFICANT OF THEIR EVERYDAY LIFE.]

Who or what is newsworthy according to a kairos mode of time? Not much. Cultures tuned to kairos cycles have little reason to value events simply because they happen to have occurred in recent chronos time. Without a historical consciousness, a sense that cultures develop and change over time, there is little motivation to see significance in what happens to be "new." Furthermore, the lives and affairs of the masses who don't directly participate in the kairos cycles are insignificant. The stage on which the drama of meaning plays out remains inaccessible and removed from most people's experience. Hence, most people and events are simply off the map of meaning.

[margin note: STRONG WORD]

---

[11]Ibid., 565.

Overvaluing Chronos

The news may be trivial for the inhabitants of kairos cultures, but for the German philosopher G. W. F. Hegel it had become a replacement for divine revelation: "Reading the morning newspaper is the realist's morning prayer." He goes on to explain that "one orients one's attitude toward the world either by God or by what the world is."[12] In many ways, Hegel is the patriarch of our contemporary obsession with the news; it is his understanding of history that predisposes us to find the significance of our lives within the context of our news feeds.

[margin note: ANOTHER WRONG IDEA OF FINDING PURPOSE IN THINGS OTHER THAN GOD.]

In jumping from the kairos sensibility of classical antiquity to nineteenth-century German historicism, I'm obviously skipping over quite a lot. But historicism's account of chronological time as meaning-bearing forms the counterpoint to cultures centered on kairos. Further, modern realism, whose philosophical underpinnings stem from German historicism, provides the aesthetic that continues to shape our own privileging of the news. Auerbach argues that realism—a serious representation of everyday life—emerges twice in the Western imagination: first, as the figural realism of which Dante is the master and, second, after European neoclassicism reestablishes a separation of styles, as the historical realism of the eighteenth and nineteenth centuries, exemplified by authors such as Schiller, Balzac, and Stendhal. The second might not be possible without the first, yet they are crucially different in character.[13]

In the next chapter I'll fill in this story by examining how Saint Augustine, Saint Francis, and Dante developed figural

---

[12]Georg Wilhelm Friedrich Hegel, *Miscellaneous Writings of G. W. F. Hegel*, ed. Jon Stewart (Evanston, IL: Northwestern University Press, 2002), 247.

[13]Erich Auerbach, *Literary Language and Its Public in Late Latin Antiquity and in the Middle Ages*, trans. Ralph Mannheim (New York: Pantheon, 1965), 555.

realism. But for now it's sufficient to note that Hegel's teleological view of history is intelligible only in the wake of the incarnation and the spread of Christianity; yet at the same time it represents a departure from a Christian account of time. As the Canadian philosopher George Grant puts it, "The modern conception of progress may be characterized as secular Christianity."[14] This Hegelian characterization of time derives in part from "biblical religion," which "taught that history mattered. History was providential and liberating, an idea that was in sharp contrast to the cycles of fortune and misfortune that defined history for the ancient Greek mind."[15] In German historicism, this progressive sense of history gets decoupled from a particularly Christian account and can be co-opted by other narratives.

For Hegel, history follows a kind of ontogenetic process: just as biologists can track the development of an embryo through its various stages of growth into a mature human person, so philosophers can trace history's inner logic as successive human cultures move toward their natural end.[16] It's as if there's some universal spirit that is progressively unfolding in human societies, and each age has its own zeitgeist that represents a stage in this larger process. Hence it is unthinkable for those of us

---

[14]George Parkin Grant, *Time as History*, ed. with an intro. by William Christian (Toronto: University of Toronto Press, 1995), 30.

[15]Grant Havers, "A Christian Hegel in Canada," *Modern Age*, Winter 2019, 56. It's worth noting that Christopher Lasch offers an alternative genealogy of progressive historicism. He argues that figures such as Adam Smith inaugurated this sense of time by positing "that insatiable appetites . . . could drive the economic machine . . . and thus ensure a never-ending expansion of productive forces." Christopher Lasch, *The True and Only Heaven: Progress and Its Critics* (New York: Norton, 1991), 52. In my narrative, I try to incorporate Lasch's insights while still maintaining that modern progressivism owes many of its features to a secularization of Christianity.

[16]Robert C. Solomon, *In the Spirit of Hegel* (Oxford: Oxford University Press, 1985), 232-33.

living at a later developmental stage in human history to consider returning to a more juvenile one.[17]

Hegel's philosophy proved persuasive in part because of technological and scientific advances that occurred in the decades following his work. Railroads and telegraphs, photography and automobiles provide the plausibility structures that make it *feel* as if we are participants in some grand drama of human development. Technological progress makes moral, historical progress seem plausible. If we have flush toilets and antibiotics, surely we are not "tribal" and brutal and nasty in the ways that our ancestors were. If we can stream videos and automatically adjust thermostats with our smartphones, surely we are more advanced than cavemen. Charles Darwin's scientific theories contributed to this sense of progress as well by situating humans as the apex of a long biological progression.[18]

Of course Hegel's heirs have fiercely disputed the precise character of historical progress. Karl Marx's historical materialism sees progress as driven by conflicts arising from changes in the means of production, and he predicted these conflicts would culminate in the proletariat seizing the means of production. More common today are various types of Whiggism, which see history culminating in technologically advanced,

---

[17]This is why Charles Taylor claims modernity is characterized by a "stadial consciousness." Charles Taylor, *A Secular Age* (Cambridge, MA: Belknap Press of Harvard University Press, 2007), 289. Lasch also critiques the metaphors and images that link "the history of culture to the life cycle of individuals. . . . From this point of view, the relation of past to present is defined, above all, by the contrast between simplicity and sophistication." Christopher Lasch, *The Revolt of the Elites and the Betrayal of Democracy* (New York: Norton, 1995), 241; see 230-46.

[18]Perhaps the most extreme example of how evolution can feed this narrative of inevitable development is the cosmology of Pierre Teilhard de Chardin, but many who would be reluctant to subscribe to Teilhard's brand of vitalist evolution still felt the symbiosis between Darwinian evolution and Hegelian historicism. Pierre Teilhard de Chardin, *The Phenomenon of Man*, trans. Bernard Wall (1959; repr., New York: Harper Perennial Modern Thought, 2008).

Western-style liberal democracies. As Christopher Lasch defines this mindset, Whigs view "history as the story of never-ending improvement."[19] The most famous—or notorious—encapsulation of this view is Francis Fukuyama's *The End of History and the Last Man*, and a similar Whiggish optimism underlies Steven Pinker's more recent books, *The Better Angels of Our Nature* and *Enlightenment Now*.[20] This Whiggish bias leads us to divide the world into "developed" nations and "developing" ones; apparently, the developing nations are going to continue to grow until they look just like Western liberal democracies! Such language implies these liberal societies represent the telos toward which human civilizations naturally tend. And this language and its assumptions so deeply permeate our culture that it's easy to forget that reading history as a meaning-bearing transcript whose significance we can discern is not a natural, obvious act; it depends on the philosophical underpinnings provided by Hegel and German historicism.

Auerbach was steeped in this tradition, and it informs his analysis of "historical realism," an aesthetic that locates the significance of individual lives and events against the backdrop of history.[21] Auerbach proposes a two-part definition of this historicist aesthetic and its "serious treatment of everyday reality": First, it elevates "socially inferior human groups to the position of subject matter for problematic-existential representation," and, second, it embeds "random persons and events in the general course of contemporary history, the fluid historical

---

[19]Lasch, *True and Only Heaven*, 119.
[20]Francis Fukuyama, *The End of History and the Last Man* (New York: Simon & Schuster, 2006); Steven Pinker, *The Better Angels of Our Nature: Why Violence Has Declined* (New York: Penguin, 2012); and idem, *Enlightenment Now: The Case for Reason, Science, Humanism, and Progress* (New York: Penguin, 2019).
[21]Auerbach, *Mimesis*, 571.

background."²² As an example of this aesthetic, consider Charles Dickens's character Madame Thérèse Defarge. If we can imagine the history of the French Revolution being told in the style of the Roman historian Tacitus, Madame Defarge would certainly not merit a mention. Yet in Dickens's story a person who would have been an anonymous member of the petite bourgeoisie is portrayed as an active participant in the Jacobin Reign of Terror. Her knitting is no simple, domestic act; rather, as her needles pull the yarn through one loop after another, they create a political document, a record of those who deserve to die. Her significance as a person derives from her participation in the important events of "contemporary history." Similar examples abound in nineteenth-century realist novels: the racial dynamics of antebellum America form the stage for Huck Finn's moral drama, the Battle of Waterloo and the February Revolution do the same for the protagonists of *Les Misérables*, and the social hierarchies and colonial dynamics of Victorian England provide the backdrop against which the characters in *Jane Eyre* make sense of their lives.

As these examples of historical realism indicate, historicism doesn't just provide a way of viewing the past; it shapes how we understand the present. Describing the development of German historicism, Auerbach remarks, in an astute aside, that "a change in our manner of viewing history will of necessity soon be transferred to our manner of viewing current conditions." In this particular case, we come to view "the present . . . as a piece of history whose everyday depths and total inner structure lay claim to our interest both in their origins and in the direction taken by their development."²³ Auerbach's description here recalls Hegel's famous letter—written as he was completing

---

²²Ibid., 491. See also Auerbach's discussion on pp. 463 and 485.
²³Ibid., 443-44.

Phenomenology of Spirit—in which he describes seeing Napoleon preparing for the Battle of Jena: "I saw the Emperor—this world-soul—riding out of the city on reconnaissance. It is indeed a wonderful sensation to see such an individual, who, concentrated here at a single point, astride a horse, reaches out over the world and masters it."[24] This moment becomes significant because it represents a brush with history. The sensation Hegel describes would today result in him trying to get a selfie with Napoleon so he could broadcast his connection to a figure of historical importance. We see a similar dynamic when newspaper headlines proclaim that someone is the first X to do Y—the first woman to become governor of a particular state, or the first Black person to become the CEO of a company, or the first union member to become mayor of a city. Framing events in this way roots their significance in a Whiggish view of historical development.

My references to social media and newspapers are not gratuitous. In a real way, media technologies create this sense of history. Auerbach points to the role of transportation and communication technologies in generating the French Revolution. Such technologies

> made it possible to mobilize the people far more rapidly and in a far more unified direction; everyone was reached by the same ideas and events far more quickly, more consciously, and more uniformly. For Europe, there began that process of temporal concentration, both of historical events themselves and of everyone's knowledge of them, which has since made tremendous progress and which not only permits us to prophesy a unification of human life

[24]Terry P. Pinkard, *Hegel: A Biography* (Cambridge: Cambridge University Press, 2000), 228.

throughout the world but has in a certain sense already achieved it.[25]

Our digital media ecosystem has only intensified this "temporal concentration" that Auerbach describes. As consumers of the news, we are invited to ask how our lives take on meaning in the context of what we are reading or watching. When we open a newspaper (or scroll through our news feed), we participate in what Benedict Anderson calls a "ceremony" that "is incessantly repeated at daily or half-daily [or hourly] intervals throughout the calendar. What more vivid figure for the secular, historically clocked, imagined community can be envisioned?"[26]

The result of this habitual ceremony, according to Auerbach, is that a reader of the news learns to "account to himself for his real life and his place in human society" according to the chronos-bound, historical narrative of the daily news.[27] The news, then, is both symptom and cause of this historical sense. As we are embedded more and more in a world of newspapers, TV news, radio, and social media, we increasingly come to feel ourselves to be part of some chronologically unfolding development. Digital media certainly amplify this effect; as one commentator has noted, "For a certain segment of the population, the news has come to fill up more and more time—and, more subtly, to occupy centre stage in our subjective sense of reality. . . . For some of us, at least, [screens] have altered our way of being in the world such that the news is no longer one aspect of the backdrop to our lives, but the main drama."[28] Perhaps we should inscribe a warning across the bottom of the screens on which we

---

[25]Auerbach, *Mimesis*, 459.
[26]Benedict R. O'G. Anderson, *Imagined Communities: Reflections on the Origin and Spread of Nationalism*, rev. ed. (London: Verso, 2006), 35.
[27]Auerbach, *Mimesis*, 459.
[28]Oliver Burkeman, "How the News Took Over Reality," *Guardian*, May 3, 2019, www.theguardian.com/news/2019/may/03/how-the-news-took-over-reality.

read the news: "Objects on screen are more distant than they appear." For those of us who live in a chronos-dominated culture, the news takes on outsized importance in our lives—even replacing morning prayer!—when it forms the horizon against which we judge the meaning and value of our lives.

Reading the Times by the Arc of History

Who or what is newsworthy according to this chronos mode of time? In brief, it's the people and events that participate in the drama of historical development. A teleological view of history makes chronos—and in particular the avant-garde, those on the bleeding edge of chronos—the locus of significance. This view leads people to refer to the "arc of history" and to distinguish those who are on the "right side" of history from those who are on the "wrong side" of history. Hence "medieval" becomes a pejorative, while it is high praise to say that someone is "ahead of her time." The flipside of this progressivism, as Lasch points out, is a nostalgia for simpler times when everything was better: as Donald Trump's campaign slogan has it, we need to Make America Great Again.[29] Both of these narratives assign moral significance to news events based on their reading of a chronological arc.

The most notable person in recent years to point to history's arc was President Obama, who tended to describe history in Fukuyamian terms.[30] When he was elected president in 2008, Obama praised those who have "put their hands on the arc of history [to] bend it . . . toward the hope of a better day."[31] And in his second inaugural address, he urged Americans to "answer

---

[29]Lasch, *True and Only Heaven*, 82-119.

[30]For a fuller analysis of Obama's use of this language, see David A. Graham, "The Wrong Side of 'the Right Side of History,'" *Atlantic*, December 21, 2015, www.theatlantic.com/politics/archive/2015/12/obama-right-side-of-history /420462/.

[31]Barack Obama, "Barack Obama Victory Speech," *C-Span*, November 4, 2008, www.c-span.org/video/?282164-2/barack-obama-victory-speech.

the call of history." "History tells us," according to Obama, that the ideals of liberty and equality enshrined in the Declaration of Independence are the destination toward which America is progressing: "The most evident of truths—that all of us are created equal—is the star that guides us still." This sense of history leads him to trace a trajectory that connects "Seneca Falls, and Selma, and Stonewall."[32]

As Obama's examples indicate, liberal progressivism makes history's avant-garde a morally superior location. And this belief in some moral arc of history is not held just by liberal presidents and social justice warriors; it is mirrored in the fear and outrage on the cultural right that lead some to obsess over each latest sign that our culture is in decline—every drag queen story hour or lawsuit against a baker becomes evidence for why we need to restore America to some original greatness. As the title of conservative pundit Ben Shapiro's book *The Right Side of History* suggests, many on the political left and right share Hegelian assumptions; Fox News and MSNBC both profit from a belief in history's moral arc.[33]

This way of understanding the events of chronos lends a kind of toxic energy to the news and causes us to group individuals into rather crude blocs. The sense that someone is participating in an unfolding narrative of progress can generate great enthusiasm and lend that person's life significance. But it can also lead to today's so-called cancel culture in which persons who are deemed to be on the wrong side of history are reflexively condemned. To return to Auerbach's example of the French Revolution, the revolutionaries' simplistic labels grouped

---

[32]Barack Obama, "Inaugural Address by President Barack Obama," White House news release, January 21, 2013, https://obamawhitehouse.archives.gov/the-press-office/2013/01/21/inaugural-address-president-barack-obama.

[33]Ben Shapiro, *The Right Side of History: How Reason and Moral Purpose Made the West Great* (New York: HarperCollins, 2019).

people according to their classes and justified killing off those classes that were deemed to be enemies of the Third Estate. Today, such conflicts between the commoners and the nobility or between the proletariat and the bourgeoisie have evolved into an ongoing battle between various identity groupings: individual lives take on meaning within a drama enacted by evangelical voters, LGBTQ activists, soccer moms, African Americans, millennials, working-class Whites, and so on.

To indicate the dynamics at play, consider the incident of the Covington boys, although by the time this book is published, several dozen "newsworthy" events will have come and gone.[34] A viral video showed a group of White boys from a Catholic high school, and in particular one wearing a MAGA hat, facing a Native American man beating a drum and chanting. This video quickly became a Rorschach test or what Ross Douthat identified as a "scissor": an event "perfectly calibrated to tear people apart—not just by generating disagreement, but by generating total incredulity that somebody could possible disagree with your interpretation of the controversy, followed by escalating fury and paranoia and polarization."[35] If one watches the video while trying to quickly place one group on the right side of history's arc and the other on the wrong side, moral outrage ensues. But if you can step outside of this framework, you might just see some awkward teenage boys encountering some of the characters who make speeches and declaim slogans and beat drums in public parks. There's nothing particularly newsworthy going

---

[34]For one version of this incident and the news coverage it generated, see Caitlin Flanagan, "The Media Botched the Covington Catholic Story," *Atlantic*, January 23, 2019, www.theatlantic.com/ideas/archive/2019/01/media-must-learn -covington-catholic-story/581035/.

[35]Ross Douthat, "The Covington Scissor," *New York Times*, January 22, 2019, Opinion, www.nytimes.com/2019/01/22/opinion/covington-catholic-march -for-life.html.

on here, until the encounter gets slotted into history's arc. In reality, the boys were neither pure heroes nor evil villains, they were neither on the right side nor the wrong side of history, yet our chronos-obsessed culture situated this quotidian encounter within a grand historical conflict and made it front-page—or, more aptly, top-of-the-news-feed—material.[36]

Those who become disillusioned with this drama—and with its frenzied adjudication of where one outrage after another falls on history's arc—may find themselves at a loss for any standard of meaning: if history has no arc, if history is "just one damn thing after another," then perhaps there is no horizon of meaning at all. Such disillusionment is a logical symptom of the diagnosis of Jean-François Lyotard, whose famous definition of "*postmodern* as incredulity toward metanarratives" was provoked by a sense that Marx's teleological view of history had not been borne out by the events of the twentieth century.[37]

A similar sense that America has failed to make meaningful progress regarding racism leads Ta-Nehisi Coates to disagree with Obama's invocation of history's arc. In describing their conversations, Coates explains that he doesn't share Obama's optimism: "This sort of idea that, 'At the end of the day, it all works out.' Or maybe, to put it less condescendingly, that, 'We're on the right side of history, and the arc of the moral universe bends to justice.' That's just something I don't share. The sense of destiny that 'it will,' I just don't share it. There's ample

---

[36]For an essay that warns intellectuals in particular against the dangers of viewing politics as "a war between the allies and the enemies of history," see Jon Baskin, "Tired of Winning: D.C. Think Tanks, NYC Magazines and the Search for Public Intellect," *Point*, April 23, 2018, https://thepointmag.com/2018/politics/tired-of-winning.

[37]Jean-François Lyotard, *The Postmodern Condition: A Report on Knowledge* (Minneapolis: University of Minnesota Press, 1984), xxiv. Of course, Nietzsche had come to this conclusion several decades earlier. See George Grant's analysis in this regard in Grant, *Time as History*, 42-56.

THE WINNING SIDE ISN'T ALWAYS JUSTICE, MOST TIMES IT'S EVIL.

evidence it might not. That's where I come down."[38] As he writes in *Between the World and Me*, "My understanding of the universe was physical, and its moral arc bent toward chaos then concluded in a box."[39] Coates does not find much ground for hope in history's transcript.

While postmodern disenchantment sees through grandiose claims about history's arc, it threatens to leave us adrift and without any standard by which we might find meaning in the events of our times.[40] In the final paragraph of his essay "The End of History?" Fukuyama makes a surprising turn toward the personal, psychological experience of those living at the culmination of history: "The end of history will be a very sad time." Why is this? Because history will no longer serve to give our lives meaning:

> The struggle for recognition, the willingness to risk one's life for a purely abstract goal, the worldwide ideological struggle that called forth daring, courage, imagination, and idealism, will be replaced by economic calculation, the endless solving of technical problems, environmental concerns, and the satisfaction of sophisticated consumer demands. In the post-historical period, there will be neither politics nor philosophy, just the perpetual caretaking of the museum of human history.

---

[38]Ezra Klein and Ta-Nehisi Coates, "Ta-Nehisi Coates: 'I'm a Big Believer in Chaos,'" *Vox*, December 19, 2016, www.vox.com/conversations/2016/12/19/13952578/ta-nehisi-coates-ezra-klein.

[39]Ta-Nehisi Coates, *Between the World and Me* (New York: Random House, 2015), 28.

[40]In a parallel analysis, Auerbach describes the realism of modernist writers like Virginia Wolfe and James Joyce as detached from a meaningful historical arc. Their stream-of-consciousness narratives offer readers moments of solidarity and human sympathy that can unite us as together we ride out the meaningless flux of chronos. Auerbach, *Mimesis*, 550-52. In some ways, this reaction to historical realism parallels the early humanist reaction to Dante's figural realism. Authors like Boccaccio and Rabelais employ a "creatural realism" that eschews the cosmic, theological vision of Dante while still inheriting his concern for the individual human person. Ibid., 276.

It seems there will simply be no news once history's arc has reached its denouement. Because of this loss of meaning, Fukuyama even admits feeling "a powerful nostalgia" for the fray of history's dialectic struggle.[41] The perception of history, of chronos, as tracing a meaningful arc is the result of particular historical causes, but it also fulfills a deep human desire for a cosmic or religious framework in which to root our lives. People long for such a narrative in order to make sense of the news and events of their time. And a Christian mode of keeping time provides exactly that, enabling us to value the news according to the horizon of divine redemption while steering clear of both the Scylla of kairos and the Charybdis of chronos.

THIS CHAPTER OPENED MY MIND TO A NEW
PERSPECTIVE OF VIEWING TIME. BOTH ENDS
OF THE EXTREME MAY MISLEAD US TO
A WRONG CONCLUSION OF THE MEANING
OF LIFE. ONLY THE CHRISTIAN MODE
OF TIME CAN KEEP OUR MIND FROM
BEING POISONED BY SEEKING MEANING
OF LIFE IN THE NEWS.

---

[41]Francis Fukuyama, "The End of History?," *National Interest*, no. 16 (1989): 18.

Chapter Five

Figural Imagination

THE GOOD NEWS of Jesus points Christians toward an alternative horizon of meaning by which we should judge the significance of contemporary events. "When the fullness of time had come," the Word who created chronos stepped into chronological history; hence, the mundane events of chronos now participate in the holy significance of kairos (Gal 4:4). The Old Testament prophets provide glimpses of this perspective, but in the centuries following the incarnation, Christians further developed ways of understanding and inhabiting this tension between divine, kairos time and mundane, chronos time. Writers such as Augustine and Dante urged believers to judge the meaning of their lives and of contemporary events by a mode of figural interpretation that locates the events of chronos within a divine drama enacted in kairos time. While this drama plays out in kairos, it continues to punctuate chronos; on a figural view, God's story provides the grammar by which chronos and its affairs become meaningful.

God's story makes the time meaningful, not the events of time makes us meaningful

When Rome was sacked in 410, Christians were shocked. How could God allow Rome, a Christian empire, to fall at the hands of pagan barbarians? It was in response to this question that Augustine wrote *The City of God*. The conversion of Constantine had led many Christians to conflate Christianity with the Roman Empire and redemptive time with historical time: "As the church came to feel at home in the world, so she became reconciled to *time*."[1] And as the theologian Bruce Chilton explains, such an identification of kairos with chronos led to a false and dangerous comfort:

> Time on such an understanding seems to be totally baptized by eternity, as if one were living in the moment of ultimate judgment and vindication. Many Christians conceived of matters in that way. For that reason, the inevitable setbacks of the Empire, most notably Alaric's sack of Rome in 410 C.E., were more than embarrassments. They shook to its foundations the faith that the Empire and human time itself had entered into eternity.[2]

Augustine's response to this error was to reestablish a distinction between God's city and all earthly, political cities. As Chilton summarizes, "Because God's city was the dominion of love, timeless and enduring, human cities could only approximate it, soldiering on until such a moment as heaven's eternity truly did become all in all. With Augustine, a normative Christian history was born, as well as a skepticism that ordinary, human time could be definitive."[3] As I argued in the last chapter, our culture's obsession with chronos tempts contemporary Christians, much like fourth- and fifth-century Christians, to conflate redemptive time with the advance of historical time. This leads to a dangerous identification of Christianity with liberal, progressive values, with America, with free enterprise, or with whatever historical force we think is on the "right" side of history. Augustine's insistence that all such identifications are false is a reminder as needed in the twenty-first century as it was in the fifth. The arc of history does not bend

---

[1]Gregory Dix, *The Shape of the Liturgy* (London: Continuum, 2005), 305.
[2]Bruce Chilton, *Redeeming Time: The Wisdom of Ancient Jewish and Christian Festal Calendars* (Peabody, MA: Hendrickson, 2002), 108.
[3]Ibid.

toward the Roman eagle or liberal democracy; rather, all its events are relative to the crucified and risen Word. And Christians must learn to read the events of chronos in that light.

On a Christian, Augustinian account, then, the events of chronos are indeed meaningful, but their meaning cannot be read sequentially. Rather, history's true meaning emerges only in the light of Christ's life. This is the result of understanding kairos and chronos as stitched together through the events of the incarnation. To recall Paul Griffiths's claim, which I quoted earlier, "The crucifixion, resurrection, and ascension of Jesus lie at the heart of time. . . . Time is contracted by these events, pleated and folded around them, gathered by them into a tensely dense possibility."[4] Charles Taylor expands on this idea when he explains how a Christian sense of a higher, kairos time "gather[s] and re-order[s] secular time" by introducing "'warps' and seeming inconsistencies in profane time-ordering. Events which were far apart in profane time [or chronos] could nevertheless be closely linked. . . . Good Friday 1998 is closer in a way to the original day of the Crucifixion than mid-summer's day 1997."[5] It is this understanding of time that should guide Christians as we seek to make sense of the events reported in the daily news.

Christians cannot replace morning prayer with the newspaper, as Hegel claims. But neither can we discard the paper. Instead, we have to inhabit the often painful and confusing tension between kairos and chronos, prayer and the news, divine redemption and the events of history. As Karl Barth

---

[4]Paul J. Griffiths, *Decreation: The Last Things of All Creatures* (Waco, TX: Baylor University Press, 2014), 96.

[5]Charles Taylor, *A Secular Age* (Cambridge, MA: Belknap Press of Harvard University Press, 2007), 55. Taylor provides a good discussion of the differences between cultures bounded by secular, horizontal time and those open to higher times. Ibid., 54-59.

recommends, Christians should "read the Bible in one hand, and the newspaper in the other," but they should take care to "interpret newspapers from [the] Bible" rather than vice versa.[6] This fraught stance is required of Christians because, as Augustine reminds us, the earthly and heavenly cities are "inextricably intermingled, one with the other."[7] Such a reality makes discerning the significance of the news so difficult; the happenings of chronos are caught up in the Creator's kairos narrative, but these times have not yet been fully aligned. Simply stating this theological claim, of course, does not clear up all confusion regarding how we should read and interpret the news. That work requires discernment, and in this endeavor we can learn from the good (and bad) examples of those who have faithfully tried to discern God's redemptive action in the news of their time.

The Old Testament prophets act as early guides in this task as they responded to the political and social events of their day by drawing on divine revelation. A Christian mode of reading time in the light of the incarnation is outlined by Augustine and then further developed in the twelfth and thirteenth centuries by writers such as Dante. Dante is Auerbach's exemplar of what he terms "figural realism," a mode of understanding that locates common individuals and events in the grand architecture of heaven. On this understanding, the mundane events of our lives take on eternal significance as they participate in the drama that is playing out in divine time. Such a perspective depends on an eschatological horizon of meaning, one that frees us from the

---

[6]This precise formulation may be apocryphal, but it does align with Barth's other statements about the news. "Frequently Asked Questions," Center for Barth Studies, accessed July 20, 2020, http://barth.ptsem.edu/about-cbs/faq.

[7]Augustine, *The City of God, Books VIII–XVI*, trans. Gerald G. Walsh and Grace Monahan, Fathers of the Church: A New Translation 14 (Washington, DC: Catholic University of America Press, 2010), 11.1.

sense of existential crisis that drives much of our obsession with the news. Instead of searching for the meaning of our lives in some historical arc, we can look for God's hand in the news of our day and seek to discern how he might be calling us to participate in his ongoing work of redemption.

Old Testament Prophets

Our modern notion of a prophet as someone who foretells the future can color our expectations when we read the Jewish prophets of the Old Testament. For the most part, the prophets do not prognosticate particular future events. Rather, they proclaim how the news of their day fits within the grand movements of God's kairos drama. As David Jeffrey observes, biblical prophets make no "claim to novelty." A prophet is not some political or economic adviser "who consults the right polls and collects the right samples so as to be able to 'call' an election, predict a coup, anticipate a fall from political favor or rise in the stockmarket."[8] Rather, as the Hebrew title *nabi* indicates, a prophet is one who speaks or proclaims the word of God. And as one who "proclaim[s] in time" the "word from out of time," the prophet inhabits the painful tension between chronos and kairos: "The prophet, like other men, belongs to his time, yet he stands for a terrible moment also outside of temporal order: one foot in the *kronos*, the other in *kairos*, his ear to eternity and mouth toward the city, he speaks as he is directed."[9] Thus the difficult task of the prophet is to call God's people to respond to the news of their day by the light of God's eternal word.

As the prophets endeavor to stand in the gap between kairos and chronos, they find themselves speaking in two registers or

---

[8]David Lyle Jeffrey, *People of the Book: Christian Identity and Literary Culture* (Grand Rapids, MI: Eerdmans, 1996), 22-23.
[9]Ibid., 28, 26.

grammars. In Jeffrey's account, these become two almost separable texts. The first concerns the "historical context into which the prophetic utterance suddenly comes as an interruption." The political or sociological situation of Israel or the threatening moves of her enemies become the particular chronos occasion for the prophetic declaration. But the second text relates God's "ethical vision" as revealed in the Torah and God's dealings with Israel. The "reading community's shared transcript of sacred memory and dream," their history of God's interaction and instruction, become the standard by which they make sense of the news. Thus, in the prophetic books, "the temporal, the *kronos*, is confounded by a continuum of accessible past and future, a *kairos* which startles and overflows the temporal imagination. The prophet is one who is called repeatedly into this second flow of syntax, and whose speaking is thus according to the grammar and logic of eternity, admonishing the finitude of the temporal, causal perspective."[10] The prophets speak into history from outside of history. They respond to the news of the day with the eternal word of God.[11]

One of the prophetic tropes that reveals this tension is the repeated admonishment that the Day of the Lord is coming. As Jeffrey explains, this trope is one of the ways the prophets juxtapose the two times with which they are concerned: "'This day,' the 'today' of our reading, is distinguished categorically from the 'that day' of the text. But the phrase 'in that day' is the same

---

[10]Ibid., 37-38.

[11]John Sommerville describes the prophetic role similarly, and he explains why our news media cannot fill this role: "We have made [newspapers] the prophets of our secular age. Prophets, you remember, were those who gave God's perspective on events. That's why they might know what was going to happen next as well as what was really significant about the past. Prophets placed events in the perspective of the whole of history. This is precisely what the news cannot do with its lack of a time dimension." C. John Sommerville, *How the News Makes Us Dumb: The Death of Wisdom in an Information Society* (Downers Grove, IL: InterVarsity Press, 2009), 85-86.

whether the prophetic text is speaking of God's actions in the past or of what he says he will do in the future."[12] The Day of the Lord has multiple referents in historical time, but all these days are, in significant ways, analogous to one another.

For instance, Joel could be referring to any number of particular historical events when he proclaims,

> Blow a trumpet in Zion;
>> sound an alarm on my holy mountain!
> Let all the inhabitants of the land tremble,
>> for the day of the LORD is coming; it is near,
> a day of darkness and gloom,
>> a day of clouds and thick darkness! (Joel 2:1-2)

This warning could apply to a natural disaster, to the Babylonian sack of Jerusalem, to the later Roman conquest of Israel, or to other moments of divine judgment. And Peter applies Joel's words to the day of Pentecost. God's character is unchanging, so his acts in various historical moments resemble one another; through this typological analogy, historical events scattered throughout chronological history participate in the drama of God's judgment. But of course, as Joel also declares, the Day of the Lord is a day of mercy as well:

> For the day of the LORD is great and very awesome;
>> who can endure it?
> "Yet even now," declares the LORD,
>> "return to me with all your heart,
> with fasting, with weeping, and with mourning;
>> and rend your hearts and not your garments."
> Return to the LORD your God,
>> for he is gracious and merciful,

---

[12]Jeffrey, *People of the Book*, 36.

slow to anger, and abounding in steadfast love;
and he relents over disaster.
Who knows whether he will not turn and relent,
and leave a blessing behind him? (Joel 2:11-14)

Joel's questions challenge his hearers to act now—in this chronos moment—in light of the kairotic Day of the Lord. "'This day,'" as Jeffrey explains, "is, in effect, the moment of ethical decision."[13] And it is in the prophets' promise of divine consolation that they provide eschatological hope, a hope not tied to some arc made manifest in chronos but one that is "beyond the tyranny of marching history."[14] The full meaning of the Babylonian conquest and the exile from the Promised Land cannot be found in chronos history; rather, the prophets insist that the significance of the events sweeping over Israel is to be found in God's faithful love and promised deliverance.

Yet while the prophets train their attention on the eternal, kairos drama of God's words and actions, they remain intimately involved in the events of their historical time. Being caught between these two times can be quite painful and disorienting, particularly when it is difficult to see the hand of Providence in the daily news. Near the beginning of *The Fellowship of the Ring*, Tolkien articulates this predicament well. When Gandalf, acting in many ways as an heir to the biblical prophets, tells Frodo that Sauron has risen and is searching for the ring that Bilbo gave him, Frodo's reaction to this news is quite natural: "I wish it need not have happened in my time." Frodo would prefer to step out of his time, to escape the confusing and frightful events of chronos. In this regard, he is much like King Hezekiah, who is pleased when Isaiah tells him

---

[13]Ibid., 37.
[14]Ibid., 40.

that his sons will be carried into captivity and made eunuchs—
at least, Hezekiah thinks, "there will be peace and security in
my days" (Is 39:8). Gandalf's reply to Frodo balances empathy
with a bracing call to courageously and faithfully inhabit the
tension between the messy demands of chronos and the divine
call of kairos: "'So do I,' said Gandalf, 'and so do all who live to
see such times. But that is not for them to decide. All we have
to decide is what to do with the time that is given us.'"[15] The
biblical prophets likewise repeatedly urge their hearers to
decide how to respond to the events of their time by the standard
of God's eternal word.

The Incarnation

When this divine Word entered history in the person of Christ,
the events of chronos gained even greater significance. No
longer is the news merely an occasion for faithful action; it is
now caught up in the divine life itself. Its meaning, however, is
to be found not in horizontal, sequential causality but in its
vertical relation to an eternal drama. Every person and event,
every bit of creation, becomes significant for how it relates to
the incarnate Word. As Paul writes, "by him all things were
created," and he "is before all things, and in him all things hold
together" (Col 1:16-17). Indeed, before the beginning of chronos,
"before the foundation of the world," God determined, "as a plan
for the fullness of time, to unite all things in [Christ]" (Eph 1:4,
10). Time is systolated around and in the person of Christ, and
the meaning of our daily lives and affairs becomes determined
by their relation to this person.

Auerbach identifies two ways in which the incarnation altered the representation of daily affairs: it lent significance to

---

[15]J. R. R. Tolkien, *The Fellowship of the Ring: Being the First Part of The Lord
of the Rings* (New York: Ballantine, 2001), 55-56.

persons and events that previously seemed unimportant, and it rendered their significance in terms not of historical causality but of figural participation in a divine drama. The Gospel narratives introduced a new mode of representing persons and events that radically violated the classical separation of styles. They claimed that God became incarnate "in a human being of the humblest social station" and lived a life of cosmic significance among common and even vulgar people.[16] Auerbach argues that as these remarkable accounts spread they formed a Christian imagination that valued persons and events that were previously deemed insignificant:

> The true heart of the Christian doctrine—Incarnation and Passion—was, as we have previously noted . . . , totally incompatible with the principle of the separation of styles. Christ had not come as a hero and king but as a human being of the lowest social station. His first disciples were fishermen and artisans; he moved in the everyday milieu of the humble folk of Palestine; he talked with publicans and fallen women, the poor and the sick and children. Nevertheless, all that he did and said was of the highest and deepest dignity, more significant than anything else in the world. . . . That the King of Kings was treated as a low criminal, that he was mocked, spat upon, whipped, and nailed to the cross—that story no sooner comes to dominate the consciousness of the people than it completely destroys the aesthetics of the separation of styles; it engenders a new elevated style, which does not scorn everyday life and which is ready to absorb the sensorily realistic, even the ugly, the undignified, the physically base.[17]

---

[16]Erich Auerbach, *Mimesis: The Representation of Reality in Western Literature*, trans. Willard R. Trask, 50th anniv. ed. (Princeton, NJ: Princeton University Press, 2013), 41.

[17]Ibid., 72.

As the implications of this story were worked out by Christians
like Augustine and Saint Francis, Christians were encouraged
to imagine how "occurrences on the plane of everyday life
[could] assume the importance of world-revolutionary events."[18]
Auerbach points to medieval mystery dramas in particular, a
genre popularized by Saint Francis and his followers, as a genre
that elevated common people and events by relating them to
the drama of the incarnation. In discussing *Le Jeu d'Adam*, a
twelfth-century vernacular French drama that includes the fall,
Cain and Abel, and other biblical episodes, Auerbach notes the
way this play links these biblical episodes to contemporary,
everyday contexts: "Adam calls his wife to account as a French
farmer or burgher might have done when, upon returning
home, he saw something that he did not like."[19] Like Auerbach,
David Jeffrey places this dramatic tradition within the broader
context of a Franciscan spirituality that employed the vernacular for serious religious matters and lent eternal significance to common life: "By Franciscan artifice, the ordinary,
physical, common culture becomes graphically portrayed as
never before in Christian art."[20] Francis's identification with
Christ—epitomized in his stigmata—challenged others to
imagine how the events of their lives participated in Christ's.
Franciscan spirituality and medieval drama, then, glorified the
mundane rather than merely seeking to transcend it.[21] The
trivia of our lives becomes caught up in the eternal significance
of Christ's life.

---

[18]Ibid., 43.

[19]Ibid., 147.

[20]David Lyle Jeffrey, "Franciscan Spirituality and the Rise of Early English
Drama," *Mosaic: A Journal for the Interdisciplinary Study of Literature* 8,
no. 4 (1975): 20. See also Auerbach, *Mimesis*, 162.

[21]Jeffrey, "Franciscan Spirituality," 20-21. See also idem, *The Early English
Lyric and Franciscan Spirituality* (Lincoln: University of Nebraska Press,
1975), 44-72.

The historical realism I discussed in the last chapter is the secularized descendent of this figural realism, one in which the vertical dimension has been lopped off and the historical, chronological trajectory made to bear the weight of meaning. Madame Defarge's knitting takes on importance because of her role in revolutionary history, but viewers of medieval dramas were encouraged to locate the meaning of their lives in the context of the divine drama, a drama directed from outside of chronos time. As Auerbach explains, God's kairos acts provide

> the figural structure of universal history. Everything in the dramatic play which grew out of the liturgy during the Middle Ages is part of one—and always of the same—context: of one great drama whose beginning is God's creation of the world, whose climax is Christ's Incarnation and Passion, and whose expected conclusion will be Christ's second coming and the Last Judgment. The intervals between the poles of the action are filled partly by figuration, partly by imitation, of Christ. . . . In principle, this great drama contains everything that occurs in world history.[22]

Because this divine drama originates in kairos time, it provides an extrahistorical standard by which to judge the meaning of chronos events. Auerbach describes this in terms of a contrast between horizontal and vertical relations: "Every earthly event and every earthly phenomenon is at all times—independently of forward motion—directly connected with God's plan; so that a multiplicity of vertical links establish an immediate relation between every earthly phenomenon and the plan of salvation conceived by Providence."[23] Auerbach is describing a typological or figural imagination, one that perceives sequentially

[22]Auerbach, *Mimesis*, 158.
[23]Ibid., 194. See also 45, 555.

disparate historical events as sharing the same figure, as typed with the same stamp, in God's kairos drama.[24]

Such an imagination values "every earthly phenomenon," which certainly includes the events that appear in newspaper headlines. The difficulty lies in discerning the meaning of these events based on their role in God's drama. The first challenge is simply our finite, human perspective. In addition, our culture's myopic obsession with chronos tends to obscure the vertical, kairos dimension. Using the image of the starry heavens, which the medievals understood as representing this cosmic, divine order, Richard Weaver identifies the competing orders offered by a divine drama playing out in kairos and a historical arc portrayed in the modern news media:

> A great point is sometimes made of the fact that modern man no longer sees above his head a revolving dome with fixed stars and glimpses of the *primum mobile*. True enough, but he sees something similar when he looks at his daily newspaper. He sees the events of the day refracted through a medium which colors them as effectively as the cosmology of the medieval scientist determined his view of the starry heavens. The newspaper is a man-made cosmos of the world of events around us at the time.[25]

Because of its dependence on chronological time, the news predisposes us to find some horizontal, historical narrative in which to make sense of our lives and the events happening

---

[24]For more on the development and dynamics of figural interpretation, see Erich Auerbach, "Figura," in *Scenes from the Drama of European Literature,* Theory and History of Literature 9 (Minneapolis: University of Minnesota Press, 1984), 11-76.

[25]Richard M. Weaver, *Ideas Have Consequences,* exp. ed. (Chicago: University of Chicago Press, 2013), 85. See also C. S. Lewis, *The Discarded Image: An Introduction to Medieval and Renaissance Literature* (Cambridge: Cambridge University Press, 2012), 98-100.

around us. But figural realism keys our lives to a divine drama, one that stands outside of and yet punctuates historical time.

Dantean Figural Realism

Dante is Auerbach's chief exemplar of figural realism. His *Divine Comedy* situates a panoply of historical figures within a vibrantly imagined cosmic order. Dante remains deeply concerned with the affairs of chronos, but he insists on finding their meaning within an eternal drama. As Auerbach puts it in describing Dante's sense of time, "The beyond is eternal and yet phenomenal; . . . it is changeless and of all time and yet full of history."[26] Perhaps the best way to grasp Dante's figural realism and its implications for how we should—and should not—value the news is through the contrast between two Florentine aristocrats and the character of Dante himself.[27]

Dante encounters Farinata degli Uberti and Cavalcante in canto 10 of the *Inferno*. Virgil has led Dante to the sixth circle, where the heretics suffer in flaming tombs. As they walk along, Farinata hears Dante's accent and rises out of his tomb to ask Dante about the news from Florence—after all, it's not every day that a living person from your hometown walks past your place of torment. Dante is understandably startled by the abrupt interruption, and when he tells Farinata who his ancestors are,

---

[26]Auerbach, *Mimesis*, 197. See also Martin Donougho on Auerbach's description of Dante's figural realism: "The paradox is that not only sensuous actuality but also history are vividly embedded in a universal frame—that of God's judgment." Martin Donougho, "Hegel as Philosopher of the Temporal [*Irdischen*] World: On the Dialectics of Narrative," in *Hegel and the Tradition: Essays in Honour of H. S. Harris*, ed. Michael Baur and John Russon (Toronto: University of Toronto Press, 1997), 119. For background that illuminates how Dante's figural realism derives from the typological mode of interpretation modeled by Jesus and Paul in the New Testament, see Jeffrey, *People of the Book*, 61-70.

[27]Coincidentally, Auerbach also focuses on this episode in his discussion of Dante, but he is concerned with Dante's stylistic prowess rather than with the particular faults of Farinata and Calvacante. Auerbach, *Mimesis*, 174-202.

the two men realize they are on opposite sides of a bitter division within Florentine politics. Farinata boasts to Dante that his Ghibellines drove Dante's Guelphs out of Florence twice, but Dante retorts that both times the Guelphs regained power and that now the Ghibellines are in exile. Before Farinata can respond to this bad news, Calvacante pops up from the same tomb to interrupt their conversation and ask Dante for news of his son, the poet Guido. Dante refers to Guido in the past tense, and Calvacante, thinking this means his son has died, cries out in despair and falls back into the tomb.

Without acknowledging this interruption (one would never guess from their utter lack of interaction that Farinata and Calvacante are in-laws), Farinata resumes his dialogue with Dante and makes a remarkable admission: the news that his faction has lost power and been exiled from Florence "'is more torment to me than this bed.'"[28] He warns Dante, however, that in just four years, Dante and his political faction (by this time the Guelphs themselves have split into competing groups) will be defeated and exiled from Florence.

Dante is perplexed: How can Farinata be ignorant of current events in Florence if he knows what will happen in the near future? Farinata explains that souls in the Inferno are "farsighted": they see events in the past and the future, but they can't see what is happening in the present.[29] The result of this condition is that when Christ returns and chronos ends, only the eternal present will remain and the suffering souls will lose all awareness.

The irony of their punishment lies in the fact that Farinata and Calvacante are cut off from the only thing they care about,

[28]Dante Alighieri, *The Divine Comedy*, trans. Allen Mandelbaum (New York: Knopf, 1995), *Inferno*, XX.78.
[29]Dante, *Inferno*, XX.100.

the life of the body and the present. As Epicureans, they are supposedly in the circle of the heretics for believing that "the soul dies with the body," and one of the manifestations of their heresy is an obsession with temporal concerns.[30] Even in the midst of eternal suffering, chronos events provide the only horizon by which they find meaning and significance. They couldn't care less about their place in God's eternal order. Instead, they're both desperate for news from home—and from our perspective seven hundred years later, the news they care about seems pretty petty. One wants to know whether his son is winning poetry slam competitions (which seems on par with asking for the box score from his son's Little League game), and the other wants the latest political gossip. This obsession with chronos defines their fate as heretics: even in hell they don't believe in the reality of God's drama.

These men represent warnings for Dante because he is tempted in similar ways. Like Farinata, Dante had poured himself into Florentine politics, and he only wrote *The Divine Comedy* because his party was overthrown and he was exiled. Forced to give up his political ambitions, Dante reassessed the eternal value of his endeavors and devoted himself to religious poetry. Yet even this pursuit comes with temptations. Like Guido's father, Dante is tempted to invest too much significance in intellectual and artistic achievements and find his worth in the praise and awards due his poetic accomplishments.

One scene from near the end of the *Comedy* gives a sense of the alternative, kairos perspective he ultimately gains. His progress through Paradiso frees him from an overinvestment in temporal concerns, and from the heights of the seventh sphere, Beatrice instructs Dante to look down to see how far

---

[30]Dante, *Inferno*, XX.15.

he's come. Dante smiles at the way his heavenly viewpoint puts the affairs of the "scrawny" globe in perspective:

> The little threshing floor.
> That so incites our savagery was all—
> from hills to river mouths—revealed to me
> while I wheeled with eternal Gemini.[31]

Dante's vision here may seem to belittle earthly news and the events of chronos, but as his *Comedy* demonstrates, he cares deeply about the people and affairs of his historical time. He has learned, though, to care about them from a divine, vertical perspective rather than the historical, horizontal perspective within which Farinata and Calvacante remain trapped. His goal is to articulate the "multiplicity of vertical links" that relate "every earthly phenomenon [to] the plan of salvation conceived by Providence."[32] This doesn't mean the events of our mundane time are unimportant, but they are all relative to the divine drama of heaven, and this eschatological horizon provides their ultimate source of meaning.

Reading the Times by an Eschatological Horizon

Who or what is newsworthy according to this figural perspective? Everyone and everything. But the meaning derives not from an event's location on the plane of chronos time but from how it participates in God's kairos drama. However, as we don't yet inhabit the heavenly perspective from which Dante views "the little threshing floor" of our world, it remains a fraught and difficult task to properly assign significance to the headlines that populate our news feeds. In the next chapter, I'll suggest two ways we can form our imaginations to better read

[31]Dante, *Paradiso*, XXII.135, 150-53.
[32]Auerbach, *Mimesis*, 194.

the events of chronos in this figural manner, but at the conclusion of this chapter it's important to acknowledge one of the pitfalls to which this type of reading is prone and to establish the general posture that figural reading should entail. Jonathan Edwards, arguably America's greatest theologian, kept a private notebook he titled "Notes on the Apocalypse." In addition to recording notes about how Revelation should be interpreted, Edwards used it as a sort of scrapbook where he collected news items that seemed to indicate the imminent fulfillment of John's prophecies. Edwards writes in his autobiography about his interest in the news:

> If I heard the least hint of any thing that happened, in any part of the world, that appeared, in some respect or other, to have a favorable aspect on the interests of Christ's kingdom, my soul eagerly catched at it; and it would much animate and refresh me. I used to be eager to read public news letters, mainly for that end; to see if I could not find some news favorable to the interest of religion in the world.[33]

And as his notebook indicates, he didn't just read the news; he also copied down items of particular interest. For instance, one of the notebook's sections was titled "An Account of Events Probably Fulfilling the Sixth Vial on the River Euphrates." As Stephen Stein explains, "Edwards used the 'Apocalypse' to keep score in the cosmic struggle being waged on the earthly stage with human dramatis personae."[34]

Such attempts to "keep score" can be motivated by the kind of figural imagination I've been praising, but in Edwards's case, it led to a rather rigid system in which his religious allies were

---

[33]Jonathan Edwards in Stephen J. Stein, "A Notebook on the Apocalypse by Jonathan Edwards," *William and Mary Quarterly* 29, no. 4 (1972): 628.
[34]Ibid., 630.

winning while his enemies—namely, Catholics—were losing. Similar partisan readings of Providence continue today; some Christians saw Donald Trump's election as analogous to God's use of the Persian emperor King Cyrus to accomplish his purposes. As one author stated, "I believe the 45th president is meant to be an Isaiah 45 Cyrus" who will "restore the crumbling walls that separate us from cultural collapse."[35] These examples indicate the dangers to which a figural imagination is prone: an overconfidence in our ability to discern the workings of Providence in the affairs of our time, and an accompanying tendency to see ourselves as playing heroic roles in God's redemptive drama. If your response to the news fits perfectly with any partisan narrative—whether a nostalgic longing to restore some idyllic time or a woke fury at those on the wrong side of history—it's unlikely to be keyed to God's eschatological victory. Christians have the difficult task of learning to read the times "according to the grammar and logic of eternity."

At one point in Jesus' ministry, he warned against being too quick to assign significance to the events of the day. Some people told him about the shocking report that Pilate had slaughtered a group of Galileans while they were sacrificing in the temple. Jesus responds to this news with a surprising injunction: "Do you think that these Galileans were worse sinners than all the other Galileans, because they suffered in this way? No, I tell you; but unless you repent, you will all likewise perish." He then brings up another recent event—a tower that fell over in Siloam, killing eighteen people—and draws the same lesson from this tragedy (Lk 13:1-5). Jesus responds to these two horrifying headlines neither by moralizing nor by expressing

---

[35]Lance Wallnau, quoted in Katherine Stewart, "Why Trump Reigns as King Cyrus," *New York Times*, December 31, 2018, Opinion, www.nytimes.com/2018/12/31/opinion/trump-evangelicals-cyrus-king.html.

outrage. Instead, he enjoins his listeners to examine their own hearts. If Jesus himself is reticent to assign the events of chronos to a particular place in God's providential drama, then we should be especially hesitant to do so. There is a cosmic struggle being waged on this earthly stage, but our human perspective does not allow us to discern all the details of its plot. Christ's repeated injunction to repent parallels the prophets who pointed to the occurrences of their time as framing the day of decision. His example indicates that a figural imagination should lead us to respond to the events of chronos by asking how these events might lead us to practice repentance or forgiveness or shalom now, in our particular context.

[handwritten margin note: USE THE NEWS AS TOOLS TO URGE OURSELVES TO REPENT]

Such questions are oriented to an eschatological horizon of meaning. Because Christian hope is rooted not in historical time but, rather, in the eschaton, the drama of the daily news is relativized and muted. We are freed from seeing the news as representing a series of existential crises and can instead take up a posture of *sancta indifferentia* from which we can respond in love, prayer, and hope. Again, this does not entail a culpable apathy regarding the events of our day. Rather, when our hope is rooted in this eschatological redemption, it becomes, in the words of the theologian Willie Jennings, "a discipline" and not merely "a sentiment." If our hope depends on our impression that things are getting better, it is merely a sentiment. The discipline of hope is rooted in faith, and such hope does not preclude righteous anger, lament, or indignation.[36] Reading the times against an eschatological horizon keys such emotions not to a historical trajectory but to God's future redemption and ongoing work.

---

[36]Willie James Jennings, "My Anger, God's Righteous Indignation (Response to the Death of George Floyd)," *For the Life of the World*, accessed July 21, 2020, https://for-the-life-of-the-world-yale-center-for-faith-culture.simplecast .com/episodes/my-anger-gods-righteous-indignation-willie-jennings -response-to-the-death-of-george-floyd-FXkkWh9b.

The prophets, for all their dire warnings, are exemplars in this regard. They have a high view of divine providence and an essentially comic view of the world. As Dante defines the genre, "comedy, indeed, beginneth with some adverse circumstances, but its theme hath a happy termination."[37] The prophets often begin by warning that the Day of the Lord will be a day of judgment, but they also insist it will be a day of mercy and reconciliation.

This comic view should inoculate us against the fear and frenzy peddled by the politicians and advertisers and journalists who are enmeshed in chronos. Fear motivates us to vote or to buy or to click, but faith in the comic outcome of God's drama frees us to love patiently. Marilynne Robinson is right when she reminds us that "fear is not a Christian habit of mind." This is because "Christ is a gracious, abiding presence in all reality, and in him history will finally be resolved."[38] Or as Auerbach argues, Christian figural realism blunts the "tragic climaxes" of chronos. It does so by "transpos[ing] the center of gravity from life on earth into a life beyond," thereby relativizing daily striving, success, and failure.[39] Or as Thoreau's admonition has it, "Read not the Times, read the Eternities." Eschatological hope rooted in the comic outcome of God's kairos drama frees us to live faithfully and joyfully now without the burden of worrying whether our "side" will win. We already know that Christ wins, even as we know that his victory is cruciform and will involve us in the suffering and pain of chronos. Anchored in this eschatological hope, Christians can develop figural imaginations that attend to the events of the news while seeking their meaning in the pattern of God's redemptive work.

---

[37]Dante Alighieri, *Aids to the Study of Dante*, ed. Charles Allen Dinsmore (Boston: Houghton, Mifflin, 1903), 270.

[38]Marilynne Robinson, *The Givenness of Things: Essays* (New York: Picador, 2015), 125.

[39]Auerbach, *Mimesis*, 317.

Chapter Six

Liturgies of Christian Time

Practice Kairos Time

In a social milieu so tuned to chronos, it can be difficult to imagine ourselves as participants in a drama enacted in kairos and so learn to view the events around us from this eternal perspective. The chief means by which the church has fostered this mode of keeping time—beyond, of course, the weekly reenactment of the Eucharist—is through the liturgical year. Habituating ourselves to these liturgical seasons frees us from the tyranny of chronos and trains us to tell time according to God's kingdom rather than the 24/7 news media.

The Jewish people followed a rich cycle of yearly feasts that celebrated significant moments in their history with God. Celebrations like Passover, Yom Kippur or the Day of Atonement, and Sukkot or the Feast of Booths mandate embodied, communal activities to commemorate God's faithful work: preparing special meals, camping outdoors, and making pilgrimages are all ways of acting out their role in a divine drama. Those who participate in these festivals find themselves part of a divinely typed history. Christ's life and ministry recapitulate these feasts, particularly as told in John's Gospel.[1] To borrow a trope from Colossians 2,

---

[1] Ephraim Radner, *Leviticus* (Grand Rapids, MI: Brazos Press, 2008), 250-53.

Christ's life forms the hand of the sundial whose shadow can be traced in this cycle of Jewish liturgical celebrations.

Early Christians followed Paul in declaring their freedom from the sometimes burdensome requirements of these festivals, but they soon developed their own liturgical year, which revolved around the central events of Christ's earthly life: Epiphany, Easter (or Pascha), and Pentecost.[2] These celebrations borrowed from the Jewish feasts and soon grew into an elaborate calendar of their own, populated with days to honor martyrs or saints. Significantly, Christmas was timed to coincide with the winter solstice; Christ is like the sun—he is the light of the world by whose movement we learn to keep time.[3]

When we participate in this ecclesial calendar, we practice our roles in God's eternal drama of redemption; we learn to keep kairos time.[4] Given the links between the Christian and solar calendars, even simple ways of tuning ourselves to the seasons of the solar year can remind us that we are not caught in a linear, sequential timeline but that we also live in seasonal, kairos modes of time. We can learn when various plants bud, when to plant the tomatoes outside, when the leaves of different trees turn colors and fall, and when migratory birds come through our regions.

Of course celebrating the feasts of the liturgical calendar is an even more important form of discipling ourselves to God's kairos drama. Corporately, churches can decorate the sanctuary

---

[2]In addition to Colossians 2:17, Galatians 4:10 is one of Paul's clearest rebukes of formulaic feast-keeping. For more on the development and significance of the Christian liturgical calendar, see Bruce Chilton, *Redeeming Time: The Wisdom of Ancient Jewish and Christian Festal Calendars* (Peabody, MA: Hendrickson, 2002), esp. 101; Jean Daniélou, *The Bible and the Liturgy*, Liturgical Studies 3 (Notre Dame, IN: University of Notre Dame Press, 1956); Gregory Dix, *The Shape of the Liturgy* (London: Continuum, 2005), 333-96; and Thomas J. Talley, *The Origins of the Liturgical Year*, emended ed. (Collegeville, MN: Liturgical Press, 1991).

[3]Chilton, *Redeeming Time*, 105-6; and Talley, *Origins of the Liturgical Year*, 90-91.

[4]Paul J. Griffiths, *Decreation: The Last Things of All Creatures* (Waco, TX: Baylor University Press, 2014), 99-101.

to coincide with each season, hold special services such as Tenebrae, and key sermon topics to the lectionary or liturgical calendar. At times, a pastor's desire to be "relevant" may lead to a sermon that is enmeshed in contemporary events and simply shoehorns a few Bible verses into the discussion. But pastors can also model a figural imagination by showing how we might understand the topics of the day by the eternal light of the Word and the drama of his life.

Personally, Christians can follow the Divine Office or one of the many variants that use Scripture to mark the hours of the day. For instance, the excellent *Seeking God's Face: Praying with the Bible Through the Year* makes it easy to follow the basic contours of the liturgical year and invites us to begin each day with the perennial news of the Word.[5] Families and friends can also draw on books like *Every Moment Holy*, which has a collection of simple liturgies to mark an incredibly wide range of events. From "To Mark the First Hearthfire of the Season" to "For the Sound of Sirens," these liturgies invite readers to habituate themselves to a rhythm of prayer.[6] Those who want to learn more about the Jewish feasts, and how they foreshadow the life and work of Christ, can follow the celebrations outlined in Martha Zimmerman's classic *Celebrate the Feasts*.[7]

Calibrating ourselves—body, soul, and mind—to the liturgical calendar may not seem like something that would change our relationship to the news. But there is a profound, insidious kind of formation that happens when the first thing we do in the morning is to reach for a smartphone to find out what new thing occurred while we were sleeping. Such habits form the horizon of meaning by which we judge the significance of our

---

[5]Philip F. Reinders, author and comp., *Seeking God's Face: Praying with the Bible Through the Year* (Grand Rapids, MI: Faith Alive Christian Resources, 2010).

[6]Douglas Kaine McKelvey, *Every Moment Holy* (Nashville: Rabbit Room Press, 2017).

[7]Martha Zimmerman, *Celebrate the Feasts of the Old Testament in Your Own Home or Church* (Bloomington, MN: Bethany House, 1981).

daily life and actions. Structuring our days and weeks instead around Christ orients us to his story and equips us to fit the news of our day into the redemptive pattern of his life and work.

Meditate on Art Keyed to Kairos

It can be difficult to discern figural patterns in today's breaking news, so one effective way of cultivating a figural imagination is to see how Christian artists have fit the events of their times into God's kairos drama. This endeavor contrasts starkly with much contemporary art, which often aspires to make some statement about our political or social context, perhaps involving climate change, immigration, or gender. Each week it seems there is a new cause célèbre—#Kony2012, #jesuischarlie, #MeToo—and artists latch on to these trends in an effort to be in history's avant-garde. Many of these are responses to worthy, crucially important causes, but they cannot be fully understood or resolved within the sequential frame of chronos, and most art inspired by hashtags devolves into banal gestures.

However, there is a rich tradition of Christian art that offers an alternative to an imagination caught within a historical horizon of meaning. Dante's *Divine Comedy* is obviously a paradigmatic example, but he is far from alone. I could enumerate many literary works that demonstrate a Christian figural imagination—W. H. Auden's Christmas poem "For the Time Being," the marvelous conclusion of C. S. Lewis's *That Hideous Strength*, Willa Cather's *Death Comes for the Archbishop*, Wendell Berry's *Remembering* or "Pray Without Ceasing," any of Flannery O'Connor's stories, Chigozie Obioma's *An Orchestra of Minorities*, Russian novels from Dostoevsky's *The Brothers Karamazov* to Eugene Vodolazkin's *Laurus* or *The Aviator*[8]—but I will briefly touch on just three that can teach us

---

[8]Auerbach notes that Russian realism has typically been more Christian than European realism. Erich Auerbach, *Mimesis: The Representation of Reality in*

how to, in Wendell Berry's words, walk the "tottering edge between eternity and time."[9]

George Mackay Brown was a twentieth-century author from Orkney Island. His best novel is *Magnus*, which traces the life of a twelfth-century saint from Orkney, Magnus Erlendsson.[10] But Brown situates Magnus's life within the kairos drama of Christ and his church. At the moment of Magnus's martyrdom, for instance, the narrative shifts from the twelfth century to the twentieth-century execution of Dietrich Bonhoeffer; the lives of Magnus and Bonhoeffer are stitched together in their common participation in Christ's death. And Brown invites readers to understand the significance of Bonhoeffer's witness and Nazi atrocities in the light of Magnus's imitation of Christ.

The Welsh poet and artist David Jones creates a similar effect in his 1952 epic, *The Anathemata*.[11] The entire poem takes place over the course of approximately seven seconds in the mind of one Catholic receiving the Eucharist. Yet Jones fits much of human history into these seconds, including the fall of Troy, the founding and development of London, and the role of the church in Britain. As Jones demonstrates, chronos time has an almost inconceivable plenitude insofar as it participates in the infinite life of the incarnate God.

The title character of Marilynne Robinson's novel *Lila* has had a difficult life: an outcast rescued by a migrant worker, she is

---

Western Literature, trans. Willard R. Trask, 50th anniv. ed. (Princeton, NJ: Princeton University Press, 2013), 521. On Vodolazkin's work, see Aaron Weinacht, "Time and Place in Eugene Vodolazkin's Imagination," *Front Porch Republic*, May 20, 2019, www.frontporchrepublic.com/2019/05/time-and-place -in-eugene-vodolazkins-imagination/. I devote a chapter to Berry's short story "Pray Without Ceasing" and its portrayal of characters who learn to inhabit kairos. Jeffrey Bilbro, *Virtues of Renewal: Wendell Berry's Sustainable Forms* (Lexington: University Press of Kentucky, 2019), 100-116.

[9]Wendell Berry, "Pray Without Ceasing," in *That Distant Land: The Collected Stories* (Washington, DC: Shoemaker & Hoard, 2004), 73.

[10]George Mackay Brown, *Magnus* (London: Hogarth, 1973).

[11]David Jones, *The Anathemata* (London: Faber & Faber, 2010).

forsaken repeatedly and finally turns up in Gilead where she meets—and eventually marries—Reverend John Ames.[12] Lila steals one of the church's pew Bibles, and through a kind of *sortes sanctorum*—opening the book to a random page in search of divine guidance—she comes to read the book of Ezekiel, where she finds a story that resonates with her painful life. Ezekiel's poetic description of divine glory bewilders her, and yet it makes a strange sort of sense out of her own bewildering life. And Ezekiel's parable of Jerusalem as a baby cast away naked in a field fascinates Lila. Though she cannot understand why God allowed her to be abandoned, she takes comfort in God's pity and care for this baby. Lila comes to understand the meaning of her intimate experiences of economic hardship and emotional trauma not through some historical analysis of migrant labor or a sociological study of family dynamics but through the images of an Old Testament prophet, images that testify to a kairos drama that includes her.

Artists in other mediums convey the fruits of a figural imagination as well. For instance, Pieter Bruegel the Elder's paintings such as *The Census at Bethlehem*, *The Massacre of the Innocents*, and *The Conversion of Paul* place these biblical narratives in contemporary contexts and suggest how the gospel might inform viewers' perspective on contemporary events, whether religious wars or bureaucratic regimes. These judgments were recognized by his viewers; the emperor whose troops Bruegel depicted slaughtering babies had these painted over with food and bundles when he acquired the painting, changing the massacre to a mere plunder.[13] A more contemporary example of this imaginative mode can be found in *The Saint John's Bible*, a handwritten and masterfully illuminated Bible commissioned by the monks at Saint John's Abbey in Minnesota to mark the

---

[12]Marilynne Robinson, *Lila* (New York: Picador, 2014).
[13]Pieter Bruegel the Elder (c. 1525–1569), *Massacre of the Innocents*, accessed July 22, 2020, www.rct.uk/collection/405787/massacre-of-the-innocents.

Figure 6.1. *Luke Anthology*, 2002, by Donald Jackson
with contributions from Aidan Hart and Sally Mae Joseph

new millennium.[14] Many of the images demonstrate a figural imagination, but one of the most striking is the *Luke Anthology*, which features parables and stories that are unique to Luke. The artist Donald Jackson was working on this illumination on September 11, 2001, and he decided to add the twin towers alongside the father welcoming home the prodigal son. This composition invites us to ask how we might respond to these horrific acts with the love and forgiveness demonstrated by the father.

---

[14]For more on *The Saint John's Bible*, see the essays collected in Jack R. Baker, Jeffrey Bilbro, and Daniel Train, eds., *The Saint John's Bible and Its Tradition: Illuminating Beauty in the Twenty-First Century* (Eugene, OR: Wipf & Stock, 2018).

These sorts of Christian artworks can inspire us to exercise a figural imagination ourselves as we interpret the meaning of the events in our own lives. The twelfth-century educator Hugh of Saint Victor held the Christian conviction that "all things and events of this world acquire their meaning from the place at which they are inserted in the history of creation and salvation." As a result, he sought to embed the Christian drama into the memory of each student so that they could locate any event or fact within "*historia sacra.*"[15] Art that portrays the intersection of God's kairos drama with the mundane events of chronos can strengthen this mode of Christian memory and train us to fit the events of our lives and society into God's ongoing redemptive work. If you read the day's news and then look up and see a print of the *Luke Anthology*, you might be reminded that you are a creature of two times and that God's time provides the ultimate horizon of meaning for your life and its decisions. Such art reminds us that the organizing principle of our lives should be not the stream of chronos represented in our news feeds but the drama in which God is redeeming his fallen creation.

WE LIVE IN A GENERATION THAT HOLDS
THE CHRONOS TIME AND NEWS TO SIGNIFICANTLY.
SO, AS *CHRISTIANS LIVE IN THIS ERA.
WE SHOULD DEFINE TIME WITHIN THE PLAN OF
GOD. WHEN WE READ THE NEWS, WE SHOULD
JUDGE ITS NEWSWORTHINESS BY THE
STANDARD OF GOD'S DIVINE PLAN &
WORD.

REBECCA

---

[15]Ivan Illich, *In the Vineyard of the Text: A Commentary to Hugh's "Didascalicon"* (Chicago: University of Chicago Press, 1993), 32-33, 37.

PART 3

Community

Chapter Seven

Belonging in the Public Sphere

WHERE WERE YOU when the 9/11 attacks happened? Almost all Americans of a certain age can answer this question, in the same way that members of previous generations can recall where they were when they heard that John F. Kennedy had been assassinated or when they watched Neil Armstrong and Buzz Aldrin land on the moon. These landmark events—along with presidential elections, public discussions of key political or social questions, major sports games, and even the viral stories that briefly dominate our social media feeds—forge a social consciousness. They do so because, in a modern media environment, such events galvanize our collective attention. It is these experiences of shared attention that create a society from a group of disparate individuals. What we attend to determines to whom we belong.

C. S. Lewis gestures toward the community-forming power of shared attention when he writes that friendship begins when two people find themselves "side by side, absorbed in some common interest."[1] And, of course, such friendship is not limited to two people. When colleagues discuss the latest episode of a TV show that aired the previous night, or when a group of fans have a "hot stove league" debate about who their

---

[1] C. S. Lewis, *The Four Loves* (New York: Harcourt Brace, 1988), 61.

team should trade for, they are experiencing the ways that mutual attention can forge community.

As our media ecosystem has increasingly directed our attention to the happenings of chronos, the nature of our communities has changed. Instead of imagining ourselves primarily as members of an ethnic tribe, or as subjects of a monarch, or as adherents of a particular religious tradition, or as inhabitants of a geographic place, we identify with those who attend to the same slice of the contemporary as we do. This book's final part on community, then, depends on the arguments of the first two parts. As our attention becomes more fragmented and more fixated on the present, our forms of community become more partisan and superficial; we affiliate with others in the thin stratum of the present rather than belong to them across a patterned, kairos whole.

This chapter will sketch a history of how different media technologies and institutions have reconfigured social belonging. Our digital media ecosystem is once again reorganizing how we belong to one another. Understanding these dynamics is particularly important because our social memberships guide our thinking. As I will argue further in the next chapter, our thinking is downstream from our communal belonging, and when we fail to recognize this reality, we tend to fall into the "rationalist delusion," believing that we can simply reason our way to truth and agreement.[2] Hence, many pundits continue to dispense misguided advice about how to overcome the hyperpartisan divides that seem to define our media landscape. Calls for institutions to bolster fact checking and for individuals to "diversify your news feed" are well intentioned, but they fail to address the underlying reasons for our warped dependence

---

[2]Jonathan Haidt, *The Righteous Mind: Why Good People Are Divided by Politics and Religion* (New York: Vintage, 2013), 103-6.

on the news and our fragmenting social fabric. Instead of looking to the news to create better communities, we should be looking to strengthen communities so that they can create better news.

The Public Sphere

The daily newspaper, like a televised news broadcast or a social media news feed, encourages us to imagine ourselves as part of a far-flung community held together through two means: secular, chronos time and the market.[3] The stories juxtaposed on the front page of a paper or sitting on top of each other in a news feed concern wildly different topics and places. All they have in common, all that justifies their belonging together, is their place in time: they are current, they are *news*. And we readers are related to these divergent bits of news through the market: we purchased the paper with our money or with our attention that the ads alongside these stories monetize. When we attend to information organized in this way, we come to imagine ourselves as part of a dispersed group of people who share only a common time and economy.

Our community, then, becomes composed of the other people who are sharing with us in the purchase and consumption of a particular assortment of stories and information. This is why we can identify ourselves by the media we habitually consume: Are you a Fox News watcher? An NPR listener? A *New Yorker* reader? More broadly, however, all inhabitants of modern society are to some extent constituted by our membership in the public sphere. Charles Taylor describes how the public sphere arose in modernity and became a "central feature" of modern life and community. He defines the public sphere "as

---

[3]Benedict R. O'G. Anderson, *Imagined Communities: Reflections on the Origin and Spread of Nationalism*, rev. ed. (London: Verso, 2006), 33.

a common space in which the members of society are deemed to meet through a variety of media: print, electronic, and also face-to-face encounters; to discuss matters of common interest; and thus to be able to form a common mind about these."[4] Whenever "people come together in a common act of focus for whatever purpose," they forge a community, and the communities forged in the public sphere are defined by its particular kind of "extra-political, secular, meta-topical space."[5] This kind of space is a relatively recent invention: Taylor follows Jürgen Habermas in locating its emergence in the eighteenth century, and it gains importance through the development of mass media in the nineteenth century.[6]

We can more clearly recognize the features of the modern public sphere if we understand what preceded it. Before the societal transformations wrought by the printing press, the Protestant Reformation, and the rise of vernacular culture, European Christendom was stitched together by a cosmopolitan elite who communicated in Latin.[7] While most people didn't directly participate in this international, Christian culture, bilingual priests and others served as mediators between heaven and earth, between Christendom and local communities.[8] Even illiterate commoners understood their local communities as participating in a larger, sacred community. As Benedict Anderson argues, however, "The fall of Latin exemplified a larger

---

[4]Charles Taylor, *A Secular Age* (Cambridge, MA: Belknap Press of Harvard University Press, 2007), 185.
[5]Ibid., 187, 196.
[6]Ibid., 186.
[7]Elizabeth L. Eisenstein, *The Printing Press as an Agent of Change: Communications and Cultural Transformations in Early Modern Europe* (Cambridge: Cambridge University Press, 1980), 117; Walter J. Ong, *Orality and Literacy: The Technologizing of the Word*, New Accents (London: Routledge, 1991), 109-13; and idem, *Ramus, Method, and the Decay of Dialogue: From the Art of Discourse to the Art of Reason* (Chicago: University of Chicago Press, 2004), 10-14.
[8]Anderson, *Imagined Communities*, 15.

process in which the sacred communities integrated by old sacred languages were gradually fragmented, pluralized, and territorialized."[9] And as the public sphere developed and expanded, the rise of vernacular literacy and relatively inexpensive printed books and periodicals meant that more and more people were able to participate in it directly. Over time, these changes drastically altered the way people imagined their communities.

Anderson, for instance, has famously argued that the public sphere created by newspapers and other products of print capitalism played an essential role in the formation of modern nation states. Vernacular newspapers invited people to imagine themselves not as members of some transnational Christendom but as members of linguistically bounded markets, communities constituted by a common language and economy. Early newspapers offered their readers a taste of the simultaneity we experience today when we read about some celebrity's death or the latest terrorist attack and are aware that other people like us are attending to the same thing. Citing Hegel's dictum, "Reading the morning newspaper is the realist's morning prayer," Anderson describes the effects of this daily religious ceremony:

> Each communicant is well aware that the ceremony he performs is being replicated simultaneously by thousands (or millions) of others of whose existence he is confident, yet of whose identity he has not the slightest notion. Furthermore, this ceremony is incessantly repeated at daily or half-daily intervals throughout the calendar. What more vivid figure for the secular, historically clocked, imagined community can be envisioned?[10]

---

[9]Ibid., 19.
[10]Ibid., 35. In his analysis of modern conceptions of time, Anderson cites Erich Auerbach's work in *Mimesis* (see p. 24, for instance).

Nations are particular instances of such communities. More broadly, the work of scholars such as Anderson and Taylor suggests three prominent features of communities that are constituted by the public sphere: they are secular, metatopical, and market based.

In naming such communities *secular*, it's important to keep in mind the etymology of this word. *Secular* comes from a Latin word meaning "age" or "generation" and referred to things that pertained to the profane world rather than to the church. To be secular in this sense is to imagine our lives within chronos time. Drawing on Anderson's description of simultaneity and the distinction I made in part two between chronos and kairos, Charles Taylor describes the effects of a secular public sphere:

> Modern "secularization" can be seen from one angle as the rejection of higher times, and the positing of time as purely profane. . . . The modern notion of simultaneity comes to be, in which events utterly unrelated in cause or meaning are held together simply by their co-occurrence at the same point in this single profane timeline. Modern literature, as well as news media, seconded by social science, has accustomed us to think of society in terms of vertical time-slices, holding together myriad happenings, related and unrelated.[11]

The public sphere, particularly as it is formed by the news media, provides a space in which community can be formed around the events of chronos. What gets lost in such communities is any real sense of tradition; yet, as Christians, we should imagine ourselves as members with all those across time who have been joined to Christ's body. Insofar as we are

---

[11]Taylor, *Secular Age*, 195.

caught up in the news, however, we come to imagine ourselves as participants in a conversation about the many events of our moment with others who share this moment.

The second key attribute of communities constituted by the public sphere is that they are *metatopical*. In using this term, Taylor is relying on two meanings of *topical*: place and subject. The Greek term meant "place," but as Aristotle's *Topics* indicates, it also had a metaphorical sense, referring to related ideas or examples gathered under a common heading. So to call the public sphere metatopical means that it hosts a unified conversation happening in many places about many subjects or issues. What defines this conversation and gives it coherence is neither a particular topic (the way that an academic discipline organizes an ongoing, diachronic conversation around a particular set of questions) nor a particular place (the way a front porch, neighborhood pub or coffee shop, or workplace water cooler defines the conversations it hosts) but a time and a set of media—the public sphere includes all those issues and events being discussed on TV, the radio, newspapers, and social media. In other words, the public sphere invites us to imagine a single, coherent (if diffuse) conversation occurring simultaneously in many places about many issues.

The third feature of the public sphere is that it is an extension of the market. The public sphere depends on manufactured, widely circulated, purchased words. Thus, it inevitably tends to commoditize language and human conversation. Drawing on Marshall McLuhan, Anderson notes that books were "the first modern-style mass-produced industrial commodity." A book "is a distinct, self-contained object, exactly reproduced on a large scale."[12] It's not an accident that Amazon, now the world's

---

[12]Anderson, *Imagined Communities*, 34.

largest online retailer, began as a bookstore. Periodicals and newspapers are likewise commodities; Anderson concludes from his analysis of early American newspapers that "they began essentially as appendages of the market."[13] More broadly, newspapers are a product to be purchased by readers or advertisers. This became particularly evident with the rise of mass media in the nineteenth century. Today, after digital technologies have developed new ways to monetize attention and have disrupted traditional media institutions, the news remains embedded in market transactions. Modern news organizations double as lifestyle brands; where we get our news signals and shapes our identity. Even those interactions in the digital public sphere that aren't explicitly monetized remain transactional—individuals post links or updates to get more followers, likes, or retweets. And the ways in which companies and governments surveil, manipulate, and profit from these interactions recalls the ways in which print undergirded modern racial slavery: if we imagine human conversation and community within the framework of a market, it becomes all too easy to think that one viable way of relating with other people is as commodities to be manipulated or even owned.[14]

Atomized Swarmers

When the public sphere provided just one rather weak form of communal identity among many others—family, place, ethnic group, religious tradition—then its dynamics were muted. But as other forms of belonging and membership have eroded, the particular forms of community on offer through the public sphere become increasingly important

---

[13]Ibid., 62.

[14]Caitlin Rosenthal, *Accounting for Slavery: Masters and Management* (Cambridge, MA: Harvard University Press, 2018).

and formative in people's lives. When we belong less profoundly to our families, our places, and our religious traditions, we're more susceptible to being caught up in the secular, metatopical, market-driven communities of the public sphere. Yet such forms of belonging are inadequate substitutes for thick, sustaining communities; they are better described as swarms of atomized individuals.

Many sociological studies of America over the past several decades have painted a picture of an increasingly lonely, atomized culture. Alexis de Tocqueville's famous assertion that Americans are obsessed with "moral and intellectual associations" no longer rings true.[15] Perhaps the most notable analysis of these trends is Robert Putnam's 2000 *Bowling Alone*, which charted Americans' declining participation in social organizations. Fewer Americans belong to the civic institutions that once knit together the nation's social fabric.[16] More recently, Tim Carney's *Alienated America* narrates the further withering of civic society and the severe consequences this loss has for the health of people and communities.[17] Such disconnected individuals become estranged and vulnerable. As Robert Nisbet puts it in his classic study, *The Quest for Community*, an individual thus alienated "not only does not feel a part of the social order; he has lost interest in being a part of it."[18] Loneliness has now become an epidemic in Western liberal democracies. And, apparently, being lonely is worse for someone's health than being a smoker. Hence, Britain has created

[15]Alexis de Tocqueville, *Democracy in America*, trans. Arthur Goldhammer (New York: Library of America, 2004), 599.

[16]Robert D. Putnam, *Bowling Alone: The Collapse and Revival of American Community* (New York: Touchstone, 2001).

[17]Timothy P. Carney, *Alienated America: Why Some Places Thrive While Others Collapse* (New York: HarperCollins, 2019).

[18]Robert Nisbet, *The Quest for Community: A Study in the Ethics of Order and Freedom* (Wilmington, DE: Intercollegiate Studies Institute, 2010), xxiii.

a new government position to address this health crisis: the Minister for Loneliness.[19]

What has caused the erosion of thick, embodied communities, communities forged outside the public sphere? There are certainly many intertwined causes, but one strand seems to be the philosophical and political story that Patrick Deneen tells in *Why Liberalism Failed*. Drawing on the narratives used by early social-contract theorists, Deneen argues that "the political project of liberalism is shaping us into the creatures of its prehistorical fantasy," so inhabitants of liberal societies become "increasingly separate, autonomous, nonrelational selves replete with rights and defined by our liberty, but insecure, powerless, afraid, and alone."[20] Thus modern, liberal societies weaken our "ties to family (nuclear as well as extended), place, community, region, religion, and culture, and [tell us] that these forms of association are limits upon [our] autonomy." Yet, "as naturally political and social creatures, people require a thick set of constitutive bonds in order to function as fully formed human beings."[21] In freeing us from all those bonds that constrain and oblige us, liberalism also renders us lonely and atomized.

Even those who might ascribe our loneliness to other political narratives concur with Deneen that part of the reason we are so lonely is that modern society valorizes placelessness: as Deneen puts it, "Our default condition is homelessness."[22] One of the causes for this homelessness is surely the colonial history

---

[19]Prime Minister's Office, UK, "PM Launches Government's First Loneliness Strategy," press release, October 15, 2018, www.gov.uk/government/news/pm-launches-governments-first-loneliness-strategy.

[20]Patrick J. Deneen, *Why Liberalism Failed* (New Haven, CT: Yale University Press, 2018), 16.

[21]Ibid., 60.

[22]Ibid., 78. Deneen rightly points to Wendell Berry as the most perceptive witness to "the deracinating effects of modern life."

that continues to haunt Americans and many others around the world. Colonialism uprooted people from their places and led them to search for new modes of community, many of which were mediated through the public sphere. Anderson, for instance, argues that creole colonial communities relied on vernacular newspapers and other forms of print culture to imagine themselves as part of a new kind of community because they didn't fully belong to either the colonizing country or the colonized.[23] Making a parallel argument in a theological key, Willie Jennings shows how colonial migrations detached identity from place-based communities. Jennings argues this detachment causes deep damage to the Christian gospel: "The deepest theological distortion taking place [in the age of discovery and conquest] is that the earth, the ground, spaces, and places are being removed as living organizers of identity."[24] Yet, as Jennings concludes, "Christianity is in need of place to be fully Christian."[25] When we are deracinated, when we no longer belong primarily to those who share our place, we turn to dispersed, disembodied modes of community. In other words, perhaps it is *because* we are lonely and detached from our places that we put such outsized importance on the news of the day.[26] Following these stories becomes one of the last opportunities we have to feel like we are in the know, like we belong.

---

[23]Anderson, *Imagined Communities*, 47-65.

[24]Willie James Jennings, *The Christian Imagination: Theology and the Origins of Race* (New Haven, CT: Yale University Press, 2010), 39.

[25]Ibid., 249.

[26]Danielle Allen and Justin Pottle argue that James Madison thought "a shared political geography" would force Americans with different perspectives and interests to find common ground; however, as Americans have come to rely on "dispersed networks of communication," shared places no longer act as meaningful checks on factionalism. Danielle Allen and Justin Pottle, *Democratic Knowledge and the Problem of Faction*, Knight Foundation, 2018, 26-27, https://kf-site-production.s3.amazonaws.com/media_elements/files/000/000/152/original/Topos_KF_White-Paper_Allen_V2.pdf.

Yet attending to the news is an inadequate remedy for the disease of loneliness. As we have already seen, shared attention to issues in the public sphere can form only certain kinds of community. Further, the media through which news circulates in this space shape the modes of community that are available. In particular, the medium of printed language itself seems to individuate readers. Elizabeth Eisenstein, in her seminal work on the history of print, contrasts an oral public with a reading public, concluding that "a reading public was not only more dispersed; it was also more atomistic and individualistic than a hearing one." Instead of gathering together to hear something spoken or read aloud, people read on their own. The result was not simply greater individualism; it was also the creation of new kinds of community:

> But even while communal solidarity was diminished, vicarious participation in more distant events was also enhanced; and even while local ties were loosened, links to larger collective units were being forged. Printed materials encouraged silent adherence to causes whose advocates could not be found in any one parish and who addressed an invisible public from afar. New forms of group identity began to compete with an older, more localized nexus of loyalties.[27]

As Eisenstein's description suggests, the public sphere is simply not conducive to forming rooted, traditioned, embodied communities, communities in which members can enact their love for one another.[28]

---

[27]Eisenstein, *Printing Press as an Agent of Change*, 132.
[28]Jacques Ellul also argues that propaganda works only in a mass, individualist society. These may seem like contradictory adjectives, but he, like Nisbet, argues they are mutually reinforcing. Thus Ellul concludes, "An individual can be influenced by forces such as propaganda only when he is cut off from

Today, our mobile society and digital media ecosystem amplify these tendencies set into motion by Gutenberg's printing press and industrial mass media. The title of Sherry Turkle's book on how digital technologies are changing the shape of our communities is apt: we are "alone together."[29] One has only to observe the behavior of online mobs to get a sense for how digitally connected individuals "swarm" in response to some stimulus: a bit of news, an image, a poorly worded phrase goes viral and attracts a fierce, though short-lived, attentional community. The philosopher Zygmunt Bauman distinguishes such swarms from more traditional forms of community: "*Swarms* tend to replace *groups*, with their leaders, hierarchies, and pecking orders. . . . Swarms . . . assemble, disperse, and come together again from one occasion to another, each time guided by different, invariably shifting relevancies, and attracted by changing and moving targets."[30] Swarms have no organization, no division of labor, no discrete and differentiated identities; each individual is a mere fungible quantity. When a community is forged exclusively through the digital public sphere, it is almost inevitably a swarm. To put this in the terms of my previous chapters, we might say that swarms are the kind of pseudocommunity that results when individuals with macadamized minds fixate on the events of chronos.

Such collections of individuals do not provide a clear sense of identity or purpose for their members, and they do not have the structure necessary to accomplish much of substance. As Byung-Chul Han puts it, "Digital swarms lack . . . resolve. . . .

membership in local groups." Jacques Ellul, *Propaganda: The Formation of Men's Attitudes* (New York: Vintage, 1973), 91.

[29]Sherry Turkle, *Alone Together: Why We Expect More from Technology and Less from Each Other* (New York: Basic Books, 2012).

[30]Zygmunt Bauman, *Does Ethics Have a Chance in a World of Consumers?*, Institute for Human Sciences Vienna Lecture Series (Cambridge, MA: Harvard University Press, 2008), 15.

Because of their fleeting nature, no political energy wells up."[31] In *Twitter and Tear Gas: The Power and Fragility of Networked Protest,* Zeynep Tufekci assesses the 2011 Arab Spring protests and their aftermath. As her title indicates, digital technologies have great power to connect and mobilize large populations, but any communities they form remain fragile and vulnerable to disruption.[32] Lasting social or political movements require embodied, thick communities and institutions, but Twitter movements tend to be shallow and quick; they burn hot and then go out. When we read only about social issues or political problems and post online hot takes, we are susceptible to being caught up in swarm behavior: maybe we'll dump ice water on ourselves for the ALS Ice Bucket Challenge or register our outrage over a #MeToo scandal or a #BlackLivesMatter tragedy, but will we actually discuss such issues with our neighbors or, better yet, actively address them in our communities? Because swarms simply respond to stimuli, they can't coordinate or sustain the patient, difficult work of love and care.

Fact Checking

There is a growing consensus that our digital media ecosystem contributes to unhealthy forms of community: essays and books that bemoan the effects of social media on our culture and decry the hyperpartisan nature of our politics appear regularly.[33] Most of the solutions these authors recommend,

---

[31]Byung-Chul Han, *In the Swarm: Digital Prospects,* trans. Erik Butler (Cambridge, MA: MIT Press, 2017), 12.

[32]Zeynep Tufekci, *Twitter and Tear Gas: The Power and Fragility of Networked Protest* (New Haven, CT: Yale University Press, 2017).

[33]See, for example, Alexis C. Madrigal, "What Facebook Did to American Democracy," *Atlantic,* October 12, 2017, www.theatlantic.com/technology/archive /2017/10/what-facebook-did/542502/; Cass R. Sunstein, *#Republic: Divided Democracy in the Age of Social Media* (Princeton, NJ: Princeton University Press, 2017); Turkle, *Alone Together*; Jean M. Twenge, *IGen: Why Today's Super-Connected Kids Are Growing Up Less Rebellious, More Tolerant, Less*

however, remain firmly within the confines of the public sphere. Such solutions will be inadequate to remedy the root causes of our weakened communities; the public sphere is simply not conducive to the formation of loving, sustaining communities. Thus, a properly Christian mode of reading and responding to the news has to be grounded outside of the public sphere. In the next chapter, I'll suggest what this might look like, but in the remainder of this chapter, I briefly examine two popular remedies for our atomized swarms—fact checking and diversifying our news feeds—and suggest that although they are well intended and good places to begin, they are unlikely to significantly improve the situation. Instead, they are like ordering a Diet Coke with your Big Mac; it may be marginally better than getting a regular Coke, but it doesn't make the meal healthy.

Many news organizations have called for more fact checking as a way to combat the disinformation and confusion that circulate through social media and hyperpartisan news outlets. For instance, the *Washington Post* has a "Fact Checker" section that evaluates political statements or claims and awards them a "Geppetto checkmark" if they are true and anywhere from one to four "Pinocchios" depending on how misleading they are.[34] Perhaps the best-known fact-checking organization is Snopes, which calls itself "the internet's go-to source for discerning what is true and what is total nonsense." Snopes has built an entire business around fact checking (a business that is apparently profitable enough to spark acrimonious and expensive

---

Happy—and Completely Unprepared for Adulthood—and What That Means for the Rest of Us (New York: Simon & Schuster, 2017); and Siva Vaidhyanathan, *Antisocial Media: How Facebook Disconnects Us and Undermines Democracy* (New York: Oxford University Press, 2018).

[34]Glenn Kessler, "About The Fact Checker," *Washington Post*, January 1, 2017, www.washingtonpost.com/politics/2019/01/07/about-fact-checker/.

lawsuits over its ownership).[35] These are just two examples of many. The Poynter Institute even maintains an "International Fact-Checking Network," which was founded in 2015 and serves to support and coordinate such efforts.[36] This work is certainly commendable, but fact checking and "media literacy skills" alone can't fix what's wrong with the atomized swarms that populate the public sphere.[37]

Our digital "post-truth" moment, where "alternative facts" and fake news go viral, may seem to pose new challenges, but this isn't the first time that journalistic institutions have tried to counter the dangers of partisan misinformation.[38] In an insightful white paper written for the Knight Foundation, Danielle Allen and Justin Pottle survey the history of the Institute for Propaganda Analysis, which was founded in the 1930s in response to the role propaganda played during World War I. If you swap out *Twitter* and *TV* for *radio* and *newsreel*, the press release announcing the formation of the IPA sounds like it could have been written today:

> [America] is beset by a confusion of conflicting propaganda, a Babel of voices, warnings, charges, counter-charges, assertions and contradictions, assailing us continuously through press, radio, and newsreel. . . . There is today especial need for propaganda analysis. . . . If American

---

[35]Home page, Snopes.com, accessed July 22, 2020, www.snopes.com; Daniel Funke, "Snopes Has Its Site Back: But the Legal Battle over Its Ownership Will Drag on for Months," Poynter Institute, March 20, 2018, www.poynter.org /fact-checking/2018/snopes-has-its-site-back-but-the-legal-battle-over-its -ownership-will-drag-on-for-months/.

[36]"International Fact-Checking Network," Poynter Institute, accessed July 22, 2020, https://www.poynter.org/ifcn/.

[37]David Mikkelson, "Why We Include Humor and Satire in Snopes.Com," Snopes.com, August 15, 2019, www.snopes.com/notes/why-we-include-humor -and-satire-in-snopes-com/.

[38]"Alternative Facts," in *Wikipedia*, accessed June 13, 2020, https://en.wikipedia .org/w/index.php?title=Alternative_facts&oldid=929607197.

citizens are to have a clear understanding of conditions and what to do about them, they must be able to recognize propaganda, to analyze, and to appraise it.[39]

The IPA developed a high school curriculum to try to accomplish this mission, but it proved difficult to find cut-and-dried rules that would distinguish normal political rhetoric from propaganda. Further, critics like Lewis Mumford questioned the merits of the IPA's "suspicion of passion"; in trying to objectively parse political statements, they lost the moral vision required to distinguish, in their case, between Hitler and Roosevelt. Hence, Allen and Pottle conclude that the fact-checking approach represented by the IPA misses "the fundamental difficulty of political judgment, namely that evidence takes on its meaning and significance under the color of particular commitments of principle.... Key collective political judgments concern the just and the unjust; the advantageous and the disadvantageous, the admirable and the shameful."[40] Their argument doesn't suggest that accuracy is irrelevant or unimportant, just that it's insufficient. More and better information won't fix what ails the public sphere and its swarming communities.

Nevertheless, news organizations seem drawn to this fact-checking approach because it reinforces their image as unbiased institutions whose purpose is to publish objective information. Yet perhaps this ideal is itself wrong, as Christopher Lasch argues:

> The cult of professionalism had a decisive influence on the development of modern journalism. Newspapers might have served as extensions of the town meeting. Instead they embraced a misguided ideal of objectivity and

---

[39]Allen and Pottle, *Democratic Knowledge*, 9.
[40]Ibid., 12, 14.

defined their goal as the circulation of reliable information—the kind of information, that is, that tends not to promote debate but to circumvent it.[41]

Lasch's point is that news organizations should seek to model intellectually honest debate and the process by which discernment and political judgment can lead toward agreement regarding prudential action. This critique of an "unbiased" approach is reinforced by studies that show that "the most factually informed voters are also reliably the most partisan."[42] One might expect that a greater quantity and quality of information would lead to consensus or at least a better understanding of our opponents' positions, but that's not what happens. Rather, "the best educated and most politically interested Americans are more likely to vilify their political adversaries than their less educated, less tuned-in peers. . . . Those who follow the news most of the time . . . are terrible at understanding their adversaries."[43] Being better informed doesn't necessarily help us understand—much less love—our neighbors with whom we disagree.

These challenges become particularly apparent in a public health crisis such as that caused by the novel coronavirus of 2019. While some facts are relatively straightforward—was the crowd at President Trump's 2017 inauguration larger than the

[41]Christopher Lasch, *The Revolt of the Elites and the Betrayal of Democracy* (New York: Norton, 1995), 11.

[42]Ross Douthat, "The Stories That Divide Us," *New York Times*, July 27, 2019, Opinion, www.nytimes.com/2019/07/27/opinion/sunday/the-stories-that -divide-us.html. Douthat cites an essay by Ezra Klein that summarizes several related studies: Ezra Klein, "Why the Most Informed Voters Are Often the Most Badly Misled," *Vox*, June 8, 2015, www.vox.com/2015/6/8/8740897/informed -voters-may-not-be-better-voters.

[43]Yascha Mounk, "Republicans Don't Understand Democrats—and Democrats Don't Understand Republicans," *Atlantic*, June 23, 2019, www.theatlantic .com/ideas/archive/2019/06/republicans-and-democrats-dont-understand -each-other/592324/.

crowd at President Obama's 2009 inauguration?—many "facts" are not as clear. While the coronavirus pandemic spread across the United States, seemingly concrete facts become subjects of fierce debate: Are masks helpful in slowing the spread of the coronavirus? Does hydroxychloroquine help Covid-19 patients? Can the virus be transmitted by asymptomatic people? Such important questions take time to answer, and even after much careful study the answers may remain ambiguous. But when agencies like the World Health Organization (WHO) issue clear-cut proclamations, only to change them days or weeks later, they can erode some people's trust in experts and turn complicated scientific questions into totems of partisan belonging.[44] In America's highly partisan public sphere, some Trump supporters saw mask wearing as a sign of cowardice, and some public health officials sanctioned mass gatherings as long as they were protesting systemic racism. As Thomas Chatterton Williams writes about this situation, "The climate-change-denying right is often ridiculed, correctly, for politicizing science. Yet the way the public health narrative around coronavirus has reversed itself overnight seems an awful lot like . . . politicizing science."[45] In both cases, people select and use facts based on the communities with which they already identify.

Hence, merely adjudicating the veracity of viral stories or political claims or scientific facts doesn't resolve contested

[44]Andrew Joseph, "'We Don't Actually Have That Answer Yet': WHO Clarifies Comments on Asymptomatic Spread of Covid-19," *STAT*, June 9, 2020, www.statnews.com/2020/06/09/who-comments-asymptomatic-spread-covid-19/; and Yuval Levin, "Tribalism Comes for Pandemic Science," *New Atlantis*, June 5, 2020, www.thenewatlantis.com/publications/tribalism-comes-for-pandemic-science.

[45]Thomas Chatterton Williams, "We Often Accuse the Right of Distorting Science: But the Left Changed the Coronavirus Narrative Overnight," *Guardian*, June 8, 2020, Opinion, www.theguardian.com/commentisfree/2020/jun/08/we-often-accuse-the-right-of-distorting-science-but-the-left-changed-the-coronavirus-narrative-overnight.

cultural or political questions. And it certainly doesn't heal partisan divides or forge healthy communities. In fact, the causal arrow points the other direction; "alternative facts" thrive because so many of us don't really belong to our places or other thick communities. As Allen and Pottle conclude, "The opportunity to traffic in misinformation depends in the first instance on the existence of distinct communities of meaning and opinion within a society, and on the impermeability of those communities to one another."[46] Disinformation is the result of atomized individuals seeking community within a noisy, contested public sphere. Fact checking can ameliorate some of the worst features of our public sphere, but it can't solve its fundamental limitations.

Diversifying Your News Feed

Another solution that some pundits recommend in response to our hyperpartisan media ecology is diversifying your news feed.[47] The thinking goes that because social media allow us to inhabit an "echo chamber" or construct a "filter bubble," adding diverse voices and perspectives will deepen our understanding of those who differ from us and may even lead us to change our

---

[46]Allen and Pottle, *Democratic Knowledge*, 18. Allen and Pottle conclude their white paper with some helpful policy suggestions, pp. 30-32. In particular, I think their idea to give financial aid to college students in exchange for requiring them to return home for at least two years after graduating is a great idea. (For why I would think this, see Jack R. Baker and Jeffrey Bilbro, *Wendell Berry and Higher Education: Cultivating Virtues of Place*, Culture of the Land [Lexington: University Press of Kentucky, 2017].) They also recommend initiatives to bolster local, bipartisan journalism. Such policy suggestions are quite helpful, but as my focus in this book is on what individual news readers can do, they fall outside the scope of my discussion.

[47]Nichole Elizabeth DeMeré, "How to Diversify Your Twitter Feed—and Why You Should," *Social Media Today*, July 25, 2018, www.socialmediatoday.com/news/how-to-diversify-your-twitter-feed-and-why-you-should/528438/; and James Governor, "Why I Started Following a More Diverse Set of People on Twitter," *RedMonk*, April 12, 2018, https://redmonk.com/jgovernor/2018/04/12/why-i-started-following-a-more-diverse-set-of-people-on-twitter/.

minds on some issues. On one level, this makes sense as a response to the "increasingly stringent partitioning of our society" that Jacques Ellul argued was a result of propaganda and mass media:

> Those who read the press of their group and listen to the radio of their group are constantly reinforced in their allegiance. They learn more and more that their group is right, that its actions are justified; thus their beliefs are strengthened. At the same time, such propaganda contains elements of criticism and refutation of other groups, which will never be read or heard by a member of another group. . . . As a result, people ignore each other more and more. They cease altogether to be open to an exchange of reason, arguments, points of view.[48]

The problem that Ellul recognized in the 1960s—that mass media led to different ideological groups seeing different articles and messages—has only been exacerbated by the way news circulates through social media.

Algorithms on Facebook or other social media networks feed us more of the content we've interacted with previously (think of the way recommendations work on Netflix or Amazon). Hence, as Siva Vaidhyanathan argues, Facebook reinforces the natural human tendency toward "homophily—a sociological term used to describe our urge to cavort with those similar to ourselves."[49] Such filter bubbles enable social media companies to sell targeted ads. This leads to what Vaidhyanathan terms "hypermedia," or a narrowing of political and cultural messaging. As Facebook and other platforms "harves[t] consumer data [and] profil[e] voters in narrow tranches based on issue

---

[48]Ellul, *Propaganda*, 213.
[49]Vaidhyanathan, *Antisocial Media*, 85.

interest," we increasingly see messages that "pande[r] to [our] pet concerns." The result is a tragedy of the commons 2.0: "There is no 'public' or polis, only tribes that can be combined or divided" through carefully orchestrated advertising campaigns.[50] Individuals in different ideological or cultural groups see their own ads, stories, and analysis, and they are unlikely to grapple with the arguments or perspectives of those who differ from them.

Given this situation, it makes sense to advocate opening up our online filter bubbles so that we can experience a broader range of views. In practice, however, filling your Twitter feed with people you disagree with or watching the enemy's TV station probably won't broaden your perspective. Instead, seeing analysis from those we disagree with tends to become an exercise in confirmation bias, reminding us how awful such people are. It more often results in moral grandstanding, virtue signaling, and "owning the libs" (or the equivalent gesture in an alternative partisan key) rather than genuine dialogue or learning.[51]

As Tufekci observes, people who read news online already "encounter a wider variety of opinions" than those who do not, so the problem isn't so much filter bubbles as it is the digital public sphere itself:

When we encounter opposing views in the age and context of social media, it's not like reading them in a

---

[50]Ibid., 155-56. "Tragedy of the commons" refers to what can happen when individuals share a common good. Exploiting this good for private gain benefits the individual, but it depletes the public resource—in this case, that resource is a public discourse oriented toward truth and common deliberation. See Marilyn McEntyre, *Caring for Words in a Culture of Lies* (Grand Rapids, MI: Eerdmans, 2009), 1-21.

[51]Jonathan Haidt and Tobias Rose-Stockwell, "The Dark Psychology of Social Networks," *Atlantic*, December 2019, www.theatlantic.com/magazine/archive/2019/12/social-media-democracy/600763/.

newspaper while sitting alone. It's like hearing them from the opposing team while sitting with our fellow fans in a football stadium. Online, we're connected with our communities, and we seek approval from our like-minded peers. We bond with our team by yelling at the fans of the other one. In sociology terms, we strengthen our feeling of "in-group" belonging by increasing our distance from and tension with the "out-group"—us versus them. Our cognitive universe isn't an echo chamber, but our social one is. This is why the various projects for fact-checking claims in the news, while valuable, don't convince people. Belonging is stronger than facts.[52]

Tufekci's concluding claim, that belonging is stronger than facts, is why both fact checking and encountering opposing voices fail to remedy the ills of public-sphere communities. These solutions presuppose that our formative communities will take shape in the public sphere, and they represent tweaks that might marginally improve how we belong to others in this space. But as long as the public sphere is populated by lonely, atomized individuals seeking somewhere to belong, no amount of tweaking will fundamentally improve it.

What we really need is to be shaped by embodied communities that are rooted outside the public sphere and its unhealthy dynamics. Our engagement in the public sphere can only be redemptive to the extent that it is predicated on prior commitments—most fundamentally commitments to loving

---

[52]Zeynep Tufekci, "How Social Media Took Us from Tahrir Square to Donald Trump," *MIT Technology Review*, August 14, 2018, www.technologyreview .com/s/611806/how-social-media-took-us-from-tahrir-square-to-donald -trump/. Alan Jacobs draws on the work of anthropologist Susan Friend Harding in making a similar argument: we tend to think against certain groups that our tribe considers to be odious. Alan Jacobs, *How to Think: A Survival Guide for a World at Odds* (New York: Currency, 2017), 26-27.

God and our neighbors. If these are indeed our primary commitments, we may learn about and respond to current events from a posture characterized by loving attention to the needs of our places and by a profound sense of our participation in God's ongoing drama.

Chapter Eight

Belonging Outside
the Public Sphere

THE CONCLUDING SECTIONS of the previous chapter may suggest that we're doomed to wallow in partisan subjectivity—there are no objective facts; common ground and consensus on important issues will erode; biased media will proliferate and further fracture society. Yet, in response to this atomized, fractured public square, many people experience a deep hunger for genuine, embodied community. Some news organizations tap into this hunger by offering opportunities for their subscribers to meet one another. For instance, the *New York Times*, *National Review*, and National Public Radio host cruises and other trips.[1] The *New York Times* promises that readers can "join . . . like-minded travelers on journeys around the world," and Minnesota Public Radio listeners could spend eleven days in the summer of 2020 experiencing New Zealand.[2]

---

[1]"Journeys," *New York Times*, accessed July 26, 2020, https://timesjourneys .nytimes.com/; "The National Review's 8th European River Charter Voyage | April 19-26, 2020," *National Review*, accessed July 26, 2020, www.nrcruise .com/; "Michigan Radio Travel," Michigan Radio, accessed July 26, 2020, www .michiganradio.org/topic/michigan-radio-travel; Anna Rueden, "WPR Travel and Adventure," Wisconsin Public Radio, November 14, 2017, www.wpr.org /travel; and "Maine Public Travel: Sicily 2019," Maine Public Radio, accessed July 26, 2020, www.mainepublic.org/post/maine-public-travel-sicily-2019.

[2]"Why Travel with The New York Times," *New York Times*, July 26, 2020, www .nytimes.com/times-journeys/about/; and "Public Radio Custom Travel," Minnesota Public Radio, accessed January 9, 2020, www.publicradiocustomtravel.org/.

In the wake of the pandemic, cruises suddenly became much less popular. But the underlying question remains: Why might individuals think fellow *Times* readers or NPR listeners are particularly like-minded and would be good travel companions? Because our choice of media indicates and shapes our identity, particularly in the absence of stronger forms of community. As church affiliation wanes and we increasingly "bowl alone," we become lonely and isolated; hence, the weak ties that join us to our fellow newsies—those who take a daily dose of "Morning Edition" or peruse the front page of the paper of record—become more essential to our identities. Pastor Tim Keller identifies this as a danger for Christians across the political spectrum: "The 'woke' evangelicals are just much more influenced by MSNBC and liberal Twitter. The conservative Christians are much more influenced by Fox News and their particular loops. And they're [both] living in those things eight to 10 hours a day. They go to church once a week."[3] As Keller warns, the brand of news that we consume can become a defining feature of our identity. As consumers of news, we are in danger of developing a greater sense of camaraderie with those who laugh at Peter Sagal's jokes or get their news from Anderson Cooper than with members of our church who happened to vote for the wrong political party. Hegel's analogy between prayer and reading the morning paper is apt once again here; when our communities aren't formed around shared attention to God, other focal points will spring up to compete for our attention and loyalty.

---

[3]Peter Wehner, "The Moral Universe of Timothy Keller," *Atlantic*, December 5, 2019, www.theatlantic.com/ideas/archive/2019/12/timothy-kellers-moral -universe/603001/. Jacques Ellul makes a parallel argument in *Propaganda*: "Obviously, church members are caught in the net of propaganda and react pretty much like everyone else." Jacques Ellul, *Propaganda: The Formation of Men's Attitudes* (New York: Vintage, 1973), 228.

If the problem is that our belonging to one another has become increasingly mediated through the media and the public sphere, the solution may be to root our fundamental commitments outside this space. John Sommerville argues as much when he describes the news as "a form of society." He goes on to explain, "For some of us the news is where we live: our identities are found in the periodicals we read and the programs we watch rather than in the places we live or the people we associate with. . . . What if we plunged into our own lives instead?"[4] There's much wisdom in this advice, and it dovetails with Thoreau's injunction to "Read not the Times. Read the Eternities." Yet, as we saw, even Thoreau did not simply opt out of the public sphere. This isn't really an option anyway. The public sphere is with us, for better or worse (or, more precisely, for better *and* worse). My diagnostic critique of this space in the previous chapter, then, is intended to help us discern how to foster healthier communities outside the confines of the public sphere that so dominates contemporary life. If the public sphere encourages unhealthy forms of belonging (secular, nontopical, market-based forms), we need to cultivate embodied forms of belonging and then allow these commitments to foster kairotic, topical, and convivial modes of participating in the public sphere. As much as possible, instead of allowing the news to create our communities, Christians should seek to help their communities create the news.

As embodied human persons, our decision making and actions are fundamentally shaped by the communities to which we belong. Recognizing this inescapable reality should cause us to consider carefully the news communities in which we participate: we will absorb many of our core commitments and

---

[4]C. John Sommerville, *How the News Makes Us Dumb: The Death of Wisdom in an Information Society* (Downers Grove, IL: InterVarsity Press, 2009), 144.

opinions from sources we read and the people with whom we discuss current events. Christians should join with their neighbors and those in need and then allow these commitments to guide their participation in the public sphere. Particularly in the past two centuries, as technological developments have made publishing relatively inexpensive, many Christians have done this by creating news organizations to publish the stories that our communities—and the broader culture—need. There is a long and rich history here, but two exemplars I will commend in this section are Frederick Douglass and Dorothy Day. Both were influenced by early encounters with books and magazines that helped them imagine more Christian ways of belonging to their neighbors. They then founded newspapers to carry on this work of encouraging readers to foster convivial, gospel-oriented communities in their own places. Their examples demonstrate the redemptive possibilities that can come when we enter the public sphere while firmly rooted in commitments and communities formed outside its strictures.

Belonging and Intuition

As I argued in the previous chapter, the news has a remarkable power to develop community and identity; it forges a common consciousness around particular happenings and results in the creation of, as Anderson's famous phrase has it, "imagined communities." Such communities are incredibly powerful; they tell us what "our people" think about a given issue, who "we" will vote for, and what policies "we" advocate for. This work of making visible and articulate the views of "our" community is so crucial because we don't usually arrive at our perspective on the news of the day, much less persuade other people to change their minds, when we are finally presented with undisputed data or read a brilliant argument that delivers a knock-out punch to its ideological opponents. Rather, we respond to events primarily based on prejudices and hunches—feelings formed in large part by the communities we imagine ourselves belonging to. In this way, the news primes our affective responses, shaping the intuitive heuristics we rely on to judge the affairs of our day. It is these almost instinctual, gut feelings that lead us to respond to a story with protest, praise, prayer, or lament and to act on this response by volunteering, by rallying around a need in our community, by writing a legislator, or by attending a city council meeting. In short, if we want to think well about the events of our day, we will first need to belong well to the body of Christ and to the neighbors with whom we share our places.

Over the past several decades, social psychologists such as Daniel Kahneman and Jonathan Haidt have demonstrated that the vast majority of our decisions and actions are based on socially formed intuitions and hunches rather than deliberate, careful reasoning. Kahneman differentiates between two "systems" that we have for thinking: System 1 is intuitive, fast, and relatively effortless, whereas System 2 is rational, slow, and requires hard work. In general, System 1 guides our behavior, but if System 1 is stumped by a given situation, System 2 kicks into gear and figures out how we should respond.[5] In describing the same phenomenon, Haidt argues that "the crucial distinction is really between *two different kinds of cognition*: intuition and reasoning," or "seeing-that" and "reasoning-why."[6] This is not a radically new insight into how humans think: these social science–based arguments for the indispensability and

---

[5]Daniel Kahneman, *Thinking, Fast and Slow* (New York: Farrar, Straus & Giroux, 2011), 20-25.

[6]Jonathan Haidt, *The Righteous Mind: Why Good People Are Divided by Politics and Religion* (New York: Vintage, 2013), 53.

indeed benefits of intuition recapitulate arguments that Edmund Burke and Hans Georg Gadamer made in defense of prejudice in previous intellectual contexts.[7] And Augustine famously begins *Confessions* with a prayer that God would guide his restless heart back to its Creator. Before he learns how to think rightly, Augustine has to love rightly. Hence, the contemporary theologian Jamie Smith draws on Augustine in reminding us that human persons are not brains-on-sticks; we are embodied, loving creatures.[8]

Despite this anthropological reality, many people remain heirs to an Enlightenment view of humans as autonomous thinkers. They believe that, as Descartes's famous formulation *cogito ergo sum* implies, it is our individual *thinking* that determines our identity.[9] Kahneman and Haidt warn that when we fall into this "rationalist delusion," we neglect the role of our intuitions and biases and hence make worse decisions.[10] Kahneman's studies find time and again that it's the experts, the ones who are most confident in the validity of their thinking, who are prone to make the worst miscalculations, particularly when

---

[7]Edmund Burke, *Reflections on the Revolution in France* (London: Penguin UK, 1982); and Hans-Georg Gadamer, *Truth and Method*, trans. Joel Weinsheimer and Donald G. Marshall, rev. ed. (London: Sheed & Ward, 1999).

[8]James K. A. Smith, *You Are What You Love: The Spiritual Power of Habit* (Grand Rapids, MI: Brazos Press, 2016). In this same tradition, C. S. Lewis argued that a proper education would focus not on students' heads but on their "chests" and that our greatest temptations to sin would come not from clever arguments but from our desire to belong to an "inner ring." C. S. Lewis, *The Abolition of Man* (San Francisco: HarperOne, 2009); and idem, "The Inner Ring," in *The Weight of Glory and Other Addresses* (New York: Macmillan, 1949), 55-66. Other key contributors to our understanding of how humans think as intuitive members of their communities include Alasdair MacIntyre, *Whose Justice? Which Rationality?* (Notre Dame, IN: University of Notre Dame Press, 1989); and Michael Polanyi, *The Tacit Dimension* (1966; repr., Chicago: University of Chicago Press, 2009).

[9]As Hans-Georg Gadamer puts it in his seminal critique of this view, "The fundamental prejudice of the Enlightenment is the prejudice against prejudice itself." Gadamer, *Truth and Method*, 273.

[10]Haidt, *Righteous Mind*, 103-6.

they step outside their narrow field of expertise: "Those with the most knowledge are often less reliable. The reason is that the person who acquires more knowledge develops an enhanced illusion of her skill and becomes unrealistically overconfident."[11] By imagining ourselves as rational beings, we become vulnerable to malformed affections and habits. When we deny the reality of our social modes of reasoning, we become caught up in mindless swarms: trying to become a community of rational thinkers, we become a swarm of atomized emoters. A quick scroll through any social media feed bears this out. As Alan Jacobs writes, instead of the longed-for "commonwealth of rationalists," our technological environment produces a

> genuine technopoly, in which transnational powers in command of digital technologies sustain their nearly complete control by using the instruments of rationalism to ensure that the great majority of people acquire their moral life by habituation. This habituation . . . is . . . one in which we do not adopt our affections and conduct from families, friends, and neighbors, but rather from the celebrity strangers who populate our digital devices.[12]

It's better to know you are an embodied, communal creature and be aware of these tendencies than to pretend you are not and be swept up by them.[13]

Those who adopt an Enlightenment-style anthropology will not only be blinded to the social, intuitive dimensions of their own thinking; they will also be frustrated and confused by the

---

[11]Kahneman, *Thinking, Fast and Slow*, 219.

[12]Alan Jacobs, "After Technopoly," *New Atlantis* 58 (Spring 2019): 8.

[13]Wendell Berry is one of our most profound writers on this theme. For my summary of his vision regarding membership and convocation, see Jeffrey Bilbro, *Virtues of Renewal: Wendell Berry's Sustainable Forms* (Lexington: University Press of Kentucky, 2019), 135-55.

supposed stupidity of their ideological opponents: How could so many evangelicals vote for Donald Trump!? Why would anyone advocate for socialist policies!? Why don't people understand the urgency of the climate crisis!? And each of these questions could of course be flipped. The French anthropologist and philosopher Bruno Latour points to the root problem in his explanation of why so many on the political left are baffled by our hyperpartisan, post-truth media ecology:

> The reactions of the media prove that the situation is no better, alas, among those who boast of having remained "rational thinkers," who are indignant about the indifference to facts of the "Tweeter-in-Chief," or who rail about the stupidity of the ignorant masses. These "rational" folk continue to believe that facts stand up all by themselves, without a shared world, without institutions, without a public life, and that it would suffice to put the ignorant folk back in an old-style classroom with a blackboard and in-class exercises, for reason to triumph at last. . . .
>
> It is not a matter of learning how to repair cognitive deficiencies, but rather of how to live in the same world, share the same culture, face up to the same stakes, perceive a landscape that can be explored in concert. Here we find the habitual vice of epistemology, which consists in attributing to intellectual deficits something that is quite simply a deficit in shared practice.[14]

Latour puts his finger on why objective fact checking or a superficial diversity of opinions won't resolve the fractures that mark our public sphere: the root problem is a "deficit in shared practice," a failure to belong well to one another. In Tufekci's

---

[14]Bruno Latour, *Down to Earth: Politics in the New Climatic Regime*, Eng. ed. (Cambridge, UK: Polity Press, 2018), 25.

succinct formulation, "Belonging is stronger than facts."[15] Neither members of "our" group nor those who belong to other groups are *thinking* their way to all these positions; we are intuiting them, and our System 1 biases and heuristics have been formed in such different communities of discourse that they lead us to radically different responses.

Faithful Joining and Redemptive Publishing

Once we acknowledge these fundamental realities about human cognition and the social nature of our thinking, the question remains: How do we improve our System 1 intuitions so that our prejudices and affective responses are more in line with the gospel? That is, how do we belong to one another, even to those with whom we disagree, in redemptive ways? Social psychologists like Haidt would point to two possible answers.[16] The first is a technocratic, system-oriented approach that uses "nudges" to prime people to participate differently in the public sphere.[17] The second answer is to adopt practices or liturgies that, over time, reshape our intuitions and belonging.[18] Both have value,

---

[15]Zeynep Tufekci, "How Social Media Took Us from Tahrir Square to Donald Trump," *MIT Technology Review*, August 14, 2018, www.technologyreview.com /s/611806/how-social-media-took-us-from-tahrir-square-to-donald-trump/.

[16]Haidt, *Righteous Mind*, 106.

[17]The seminal work here is Richard H. Thaler and Cass R. Sunstein, *Nudge: Improving Decisions About Health, Wealth, and Happiness*, rev. & exp. ed. (New York: Penguin, 2009). Haidt also cites the Heaths' book on this topic: Chip Heath and Dan Heath, *Switch: How to Change Things When Change Is Hard* (New York: Crown, 2010). For a list of promising policy proposals that could helpfully "nudge" the way we participate in the public sphere, see Allen and Pottle, *Democratic Knowledge*, 30-32.

[18]There have been a wealth of books and essays published in the past decade that apply this approach to the Christian life. See, for example, Jonathan Brooks, *Church Forsaken: Practicing Presence in Neglected Neighborhoods*, foreword by Sho Baraka (Downers Grove, IL: InterVarsity Press, 2018); Justin Whitmel Earley, *The Common Rule: Habits of Purpose for an Age of Distraction* (Downers Grove, IL: InterVarsity Press, 2019); James K. A. Smith, *Desiring the Kingdom: Worship, Worldview, and Cultural Formation*, Cultural Liturgies 1 (Grand Rapids, MI: Baker Academic, 2009); and Tish Harrison

but as this book is written primarily for consumers of the news rather than journalists or policymakers, my focus is on the latter approach. This is why each of the book's three parts concludes with practices that can reorient the ways our engagement with the news forms our attention, our sense of time, and our belonging.

In many ways, this section on belonging is the trump card: the most formative practices we engage in, particularly with regard to reading and discussing the news, are those practices that join us to other people and so define our communities. The company we keep and the topics of conversation we share with them determine our affective response to the news and shape the conclusions we come to. Kahneman puts the matter bluntly: "For some of our most important beliefs we have no evidence at all, except that people we love and trust hold these beliefs."[19] In their work on the formation of factions and partisanship, Danielle Allen and Justin Pottle similarly note, "Our reasoning shortcuts . . . grow out of our immediate social environments. . . . In other words, our various forms of shortcuts are not idiosyncratic; . . . they are social."[20] The upshot of all this is that, as Alan Jacobs argues, we should take very seriously who we

---

Warren, *Liturgy of the Ordinary: Sacred Practices in Everyday Life* (Downers Grove, IL: InterVarsity Press, 2016).

[19]Kahneman, *Thinking, Fast and Slow*, 209. Paul Griffiths makes a related case, claiming that "ordinarily, . . . argument is not an instrument of any significance in bringing people to conviction about [political policies]. . . . You believe what you believe about these things, ordinarily, on the twin grounds of authoritative testimony and the formatively persuasive power of the company you keep." Paul J. Griffiths, *Decreation: The Last Things of All Creatures* (Waco, TX: Baylor University Press, 2014), 344.

[20]Allen and Pottle, *Democratic Knowledge*, 16. Also focusing on the political arena, Haidt points out that voters make choices not as self-interested individuals but as members of particular groups: studies that analyze voting patterns have found that "people care about their groups, whether those be racial, regional, religious, or political. . . . Our politics is groupish, not selfish." Haidt, *Righteous Mind*, 100; see also 220-21.

spend time with and think alongside: "Learning to *feel* as we should is enormously helpful for learning to *think* as we should. And this is why learning to think with the best people, and *not* to think with the worst, is so important. To dwell habitually with people is inevitably to adopt their way of approaching the world, which is a matter not just of ideas but also of practices."[21]

In general terms, there are two sets of practices that can help us feel and think within healthy communities. The first category entails practices of joining that root our identity in embodied communities. The second category entails participating in the media in ways that counter the particular, warping pressures of the public sphere.

Faithful joining. Most fundamentally, healing the tribalism that marks our media ecology will require Christians to take up what Willie Jennings calls the "incarnational practice" of "joining," the act of crossing racial or class or economic or ideological divides to belong with our fellow Christians and with our neighbors.[22] Jennings offers a rich theology of joining, one that relies on recognizing place as an opportunity for redemptive engagement: "The space of communion is always ready to appear where the people of God reach down to join the land and reach out to join those around them, their near and distant neighbors."[23] Jennings challenges Christians whose communities have been fractured and marred by racism, pride, or selfishness to take up the work of joining—to move into a neighborhood, worship on Sunday morning, or grow a garden with people who don't look like you. Such work will not result in perfect agreement about all issues; instead, it will

---

[21]Alan Jacobs, *How to Think: A Survival Guide for a World at Odds* (New York: Currency, 2017), 87.
[22]Willie James Jennings, *The Christian Imagination: Theology and the Origins of Race* (New Haven, CT: Yale University Press, 2010), 113.
[23]Ibid.

lead to empathy for those with whom we disagree but to whom we now belong.[24]

This work of joining can form us to enter the public sphere in more redemptive ways. It does this by reshaping the directionality of our allegiances: Is our belonging in the public sphere dictating our interactions with our fellow church members, relatives, and neighbors, or are we entering the public sphere on the basis of our commitments to our neighbors, the least of these in our community, and our fellow parishioners? Obviously there will be mutual influence: the stories we read in our news feed will affect our worship and our conversations with relatives or coworkers. But if we imagine ourselves as members of embodied communities, we will be better equipped to enter the public sphere redemptively while resisting its particular warping pressures. The key question is, What imagined community shapes our engagement with the news? If our primary allegiance is to our swarm in the public sphere, we will be tempted to grandstand, signal our virtues, or "own the libs" (and we may want to get away from our benighted neighbors and go on vacation with those who consume our preferred brand of news). If, however, we belong primarily to our places, we might wonder how a new citizenship policy will affect our immigrant neighbor, or how a new bus schedule could improve the lives of our neighbors who don't have cars.

---

[24]Charles Taylor makes a related point when he argues that the stance of objective disengagement is not an effective way to understand someone coming from a radically different perspective: "When we want to understand what someone is trying to tell us in a conversation; or to grasp what motivates some person or group, how they see the world, and what kinds of things are important to them, disengagement will almost certainly be a self-stultifying strategy. We have to be open to the person or event, allowing our responses to meaning full reign, which generally means our feelings, which reflect these responses." Charles Taylor, *A Secular Age* (Cambridge, MA: Belknap Press of Harvard University Press, 2007), 285.

Such belonging shapes both how we read the news and how we might ourselves speak into the public sphere. Wendell Berry's poem "To a Siberian Woodsman" provides a good example here, particularly as it also shows how belonging to our places affects our engagement with international events. The poem was published during the Vietnam War (and, of course, the ongoing Cold War), and Berry explicitly frames it as a response to "looking at some pictures in a magazine"; he's modeling one way of responding to a distant news story. Instead of imagining himself as an abstract American citizen confronting a generic Russian, Berry imagines himself "here in Kentucky" as a father and a farmer reading about another father who, like Berry, fishes with his son, eats with his family, works in the woods, and delights in the beauty of the forest. Because both the poet and the Siberian woodsman belong to their respective places, they have much in common, and so Berry asks, "Who has invented our enmity?"[25] Berry's commitments to his place do not lead him to opt out of the public sphere; rather, his participation in this space is shaped by his love for his neighbors and his theological convictions regarding pacifism. In fact, because he is speaking from these commitments, his poem works against the grain of the very public sphere it participates in.

Redemptive publishing. In this regard, Berry's poem is one small gesture within a much broader tradition of Christians seeking to enter the public sphere while remaining firmly rooted in embodied, theological communities. Christians have long been early adopters of new communications technologies because they've recognized the ways that these tools—Gutenberg's printing press, the industrial printing

---

[25]Wendell Berry, *New Collected Poems* (Berkeley, CA: Counterpoint, 2012), 107-9.

methods of the nineteenth century, radio, TV, and now the internet—provide incredible opportunities to raise public consciousness about important issues and topics; to bind people together around shared attention to important issues of the day; and to inspire acts of mercy, redemptive work, and prayer.

While the first decades of the third millennium have not been good for traditional media organizations or, in many respects, the overall state of our public sphere, small new media organizations doing good work abound. The proliferation of websites, podcasts, community newsletters, small print quarterlies, and local papers is, overall, a promising development. It's true that digital technologies can amplify fringe voices and enable toxic communities to spread their messages. Nevertheless, we can't simply try to erase such voices and get everyone to listen to the same three broadcast TV networks or subscribe to the same "centrist" newspapers. America of the 1950s was a weird anomaly, and while we may long for the sense of civic unity that we associate with that era, we shouldn't be nostalgic for a bland, monochromatic public discourse. The only answer to the toxic communities that form through digital media—from the more extreme ones like White nationalists to the garden-variety echo chambers of our social media feeds—is not to seek to flatten the public sphere but to foster rich, vibrant, lively communities of discourse.

Redemptive Christian news organizations and authors find ways to subvert the deformative dynamics of the public sphere. They labor along the margins of a broken system, making do as best they can to inspire and equip readers to belong more faithfully to their own places and people.[26] Whereas conversations

---

[26]For a theoretical—and implicitly theological—account of the power of "making do" along the margins of oppressive systems, see Michel de Certeau, *The Practice of Everyday Life*, trans. Steven Rendall (Berkeley: University of California Press, 2011).

in the public sphere tend to be secular, nontopical, and market based, these people and organizations host kairotic, topical, and convivial discussions. By *kairotic*, I mean that they publish evergreen stories and avoid being caught up in the topic du jour; their horizon of significance is the arc of the Christian narrative rather than the 24/7 news cycle. One example of this would be the nonprofit profiles that *World* magazine publishes each year for its Hope Awards.[27] By topical, I mean that they don't try to cover every issue or give equal space to all perspectives. Instead, they have an orienting mission, one rooted in the gospel or even a specific facet of the gospel. As I'll discuss below, Frederick Douglass's papers were committed to the abolition of slavery, and Dorothy Day's *Catholic Worker* has traditionally focused on labor issues and pacifism. Such work is oriented by particular commitments rooted outside the public sphere. Finally, by convivial, I mean that these organizations are not chasing subscribers and advertisers but are instead cultivating a community of discourse among their readers. Paradigmatic examples include *Catholic Worker* and *Plough Quarterly*, which is published by the Anabaptist Bruderhof community; these publications are published by Christians who actually live together.[28] But many other publications hold conferences and gatherings, host private Facebook groups, or find other ways to foster genuine community among their readers and contributors. Participating in these news communities will shape our intuitions so that we are more likely to respond to stories and events with love rather than outrage, prayer rather than bitterness, and embodied action rather than telescopic morality.

---

[27]"Directory of Hope Awards Finalists," *World*, accessed July 20, 2020, https://world.wng.org/content/directory_of_hope_awards_finalists.

[28]FAQs, Catholic Worker Movement, accessed July 27, 2020, www.catholicworker.org; and Home page, *Plough*, accessed July 27, 2020, www.plough.com/en.

Frederick Douglass

Looking at some exemplars might help us envision what a healthy interplay between media and community can look like. While there are many people I could highlight as models of faithful belonging and redemptive publishing, it would be hard to top Frederick Douglass and Dorothy Day. For both of them, reading books and newspapers transformed their lives, introducing them to new communities of discourse and action. Their reading led them to imagine new possibilities for joining with and working among the members of their own places. This membership, in turn, led them to speak publicly on behalf of their communities, challenging others to belong redemptively to their own neighbors and to address the pressing issues of their time.

In his autobiography, Douglass describes the arduous process by which he learned to read, first through the good graces of a naive slave mistress, and then by giving poor White boys bread in exchange for lessons. At the age of twelve, he read *The Columbian Orator*, a classroom anthology of speeches and poems that includes an imagined dialogue between a master and his slave. The slave made such good arguments for his emancipation that the master granted his manumission. Douglass was, of course, drawn to these arguments: "They gave tongue to interesting thoughts of my own soul, which had frequently flashed through my mind, and died away for want of utterance." As Douglass goes on to explain, he didn't even know the meaning of the word *abolition*—much less that there was a whole community of abolitionists agitating for the end of slavery—until he read a newspaper account of abolitionist activities.[29]

---

[29]Frederick Douglass and Harriet Jacobs, *Narrative of the Life of Frederick Douglass, an American Slave & Incidents in the Life of a Slave Girl*, intro. Kwame Anthony Appiah (New York: Random House, 2004), 48-52; see also David W. Blight, *Frederick Douglass: Prophet of Freedom* (New York: Simon & Schuster, 2020), 43-47.

After his reading brought the abolition community to his consciousness and helped him articulate a case for emancipation, Douglass devoted his energies to educating his enslaved friends. Once he had "created in them a strong desire to learn how to read," he held a Sabbath school and taught any enslaved people who were interested. Their school was eventually discovered and broken up by White masters; these men knew the grave danger that reading posed to the institution of slavery. As Douglass testifies, this learning community provided a rare opportunity for these downtrodden people to behave like "intellectual, moral, and accountable beings."[30] Eventually, Douglass escaped to the north, but instead of feeling free, he felt terribly lonely and vulnerable.[31] He was particularly grateful for the aid of other free Black persons and abolitionists who helped him find a home in New Bedford.

This community, and the support it provided for its vulnerable members, motivated Douglass to take a more active role in sustaining it. He describes an incident where a free Black person had a dispute with a fugitive and threatened to betray him; the entire community came together to send the traitor away and protect the fugitive. It is this camaraderie and solidarity that inspired Douglass to move into the public sphere and advocate for the abolition of slavery and the empowerment of free African Americans. He tells of his joy when he was able to pay for a subscription to the *Liberator*, William Lloyd Garrison's abolitionist paper. This paper, Douglass attests, "became my meat and my drink. My soul was set all on fire." And it soon gave him an "idea of the principles, measures, and spirit of the anti-slavery reform." At the urging of others, he began to speak at churches and abolitionist meetings, and his eloquence and testimony soon made him a popular speaker.[32]

---

[30]Douglass and Jacobs, *Narrative of the Life of Frederick Douglass*, 84.
[31]Ibid., 105.
[32]Ibid., 112.

Douglass eventually separated himself from Garrison's paper and speaking circuit and founded his own newspaper, the *North Star*. In the opening editorial, he situates the paper as a communal endeavor, arguing that the Black community "must be our own representatives and advocates, not exclusively, but peculiarly—not distinct from, but in connection with our white friends."[33] Thus it will not be committed to an ideology but to a community, which he names as "our long oppressed and plundered fellow countrymen": "We shall cordially approve every measure and effort calculated to advance your sacred cause, and strenuously oppose any which in our opinion may tend to retard its progress." Rather than being narrowly antislavery, it will also discuss issues such as "Temperance, Peace, Capital Punishment, Education. . . . While advocating your rights, the *North Star* will strive to throw light on your duties. [W]hile it will not fail to make known your virtues, it will not shun to discover your faults. To be faithful to our foes it must be faithful to ourselves, in all things."[34] This language of rights and duties is common in republican discourse, but it emphasizes that Douglass was committed not just to an ideology or an interest group but to the formation of a healthy community.

Though he disagreed with Garrison about the best political strategy to achieve abolition, Douglass shared Garrison's religious convictions. One version of the *Liberator*'s masthead depicts Christ in his role as liberator, proclaiming, "I come to break the bonds of the oppressor." Similarly, the motto of Douglass's *North Star* declares, "Right is of no sex—Truth is of no color—God is the Father of us all, and all we are brethren." If Douglass belonged to his fellow oppressed countrymen (and

[33]Frederick Douglass, "Our Paper and Its Prospects," *North Star*, December 3, 1847.
[34]Frederick Douglass, "To Our Oppressed Countrymen," *North Star*, December 3, 1847.

Figure 8.1. The masthead of William Lloyd Garrison's *The Liberator*, 1861

women—he was an early supporter of the suffrage movement), he belonged equally to the biblical prophetic tradition. As his biographer David Blight puts it, "Douglass not only used the Hebrew prophets; he joined them." Douglass consistently "rooted his own story and especially the story of African Americans in the oldest and most powerful stories of the Hebrew prophets."[35] Douglass's political and social advocacy is unintelligible without a theological understanding of the fatherhood of God and the brotherhood of all people.

Ultimately, Douglass strove to build a community keyed to the gospel rather than to political trends. He failed at times, getting drawn into heated and sometimes petty political disputes and caring more about wielding political power than about standing as a faithful witness, but the very existence of his papers helped people imagine a community of Christians committed to living out the gospel's valuation of each person—regardless of their race—as a child of God.[36] Papers like the *North Star* can help us see those neighbors whom we might otherwise overlook; they can help us imagine ourselves as

---

[35]Blight, *Frederick Douglass*, 228, xvii. See also D. H. Dilbeck, *Frederick Douglass: America's Prophet* (Chapel Hill: University of North Carolina Press, 2018).

[36]Blight, *Frederick Douglass*, 217-27; 537. On Douglass's shift from prophetic outsider to government insider, see also Cornel West and Christa Buschendorf, *Black Prophetic Fire* (Boston: Beacon Press, 2015), 13-36.

members of a community that cares about the plight of the enslaved and others who are oppressed and that takes action to participate in God's ongoing redemptive work.

Dorothy Day

Dorothy Day was born two years after Douglass died, and while she worked in a different era and context than Douglass did, her involvement with publishing and the news followed a similar arc. As a young woman, she worked for various socialist newspapers and became involved in labor activism. Yet, while she was finding her identity in these political causes, she was also drawn by the Christian vision of authors like Thomas à Kempis, Augustine, and the contributors to the Catholic magazine *Messenger of the Sacred Heart*. She particularly credits "Dostoyevsky [and] Huysmans (what different men!)" as giving her the "desire and background" to join the church.[37]

As a new Catholic, Day felt distanced from her former socialist associates—who were mostly atheists—but also frustrated by the lack of concern her Catholic friends had for the poor. These fraught emotions came to a head in the depths of the Great Depression while watching a 1932 workers' march through Washington, DC, that called for labor-friendly laws. She longed for Christians to step up and interpret these class conflicts differently, not as a communist revolution against freedom but as the cry of the poor and downtrodden, of those who are close to God: "How our dear Lord must love them, I kept thinking to myself. They were His friends, His comrades, and who knows how close to His heart in their attempt to work for justice."[38] It was on her return to New York from reporting

---

[37]Dorothy Day, *The Long Loneliness: The Autobiography of the Legendary Catholic Social Activist* (San Francisco: HarperCollins, 1997), 142.
[38]Ibid., 165.

on this march that she found Peter Maurin waiting for her in her apartment. Maurin's unified vision guided her as she worked to bring together the two communities she identified with: workers and Catholics.

The *Catholic Worker* sparked and fed what become the Catholic Worker Movement, which included not only the newspaper but "houses of hospitality" and farms across the country. Day and Maurin refused to separate the work of feeding the poor and tending the sick from the work of writing, printing, and distributing the newspaper. And in fact many of the poor who came to them for aid ended up helping with the tasks required to make and sell the paper.[39] These motley origins were reflected in the paper's diverse features. It included muckraking and investigative stories on particular issues—strikes, Arkansas sharecroppers, and tenant evictions—as well as more theoretical, theological pieces.[40] The paper also functioned as a kind of Catholic Worker newsletter, including announcements related to various Catholic Worker houses.

The paper, the houses of hospitality, the acts of mercy—these were Day's means of ameliorating the loneliness and alienation that mark human life, particularly in an industrial society: "We have all known the long loneliness and we have learned that the only solution is love and that love comes with community."[41] From her own experience, Day had learned that newspapers could help form convivial communities, and she devoted her life to a work that would combine faithful joining with redemptive publishing. Day didn't aspire to become a "thought leader" with a prominent "platform"; she cultivated a community

---

[39]Ibid., 182-204.

[40]Nancy L. Roberts, "Dorothy Day: Editor and Advocacy Journalist," in *Revolution of the Heart: Essays on the Catholic Worker*, ed. Patrick Coy (Philadelphia: Temple University Press, 1988), 115-33.

[41]Day, *Long Loneliness*, 286.

and committed herself to the unglamorous, difficult work of institution building.

Douglass and Day were two of the greatest advocacy journalists in American history. Both joined themselves to other Christians—particularly the oppressed and marginalized—and then sought to create the news from the perspective of these communities. Subscribers who read issue after issue of one of their papers could gradually come to belong to a readerly community and begin to imagine more faithful ways of joining with others in their own places. Reading such papers—and writing essays or letters, donating funds, and discussing the stories—becomes a shared practice, a formative liturgy, that aligns readers' affective responses with the gospel. Through these papers, then, Douglass and Day helped their readers participate in the public sphere, not as atomized individuals swarming around titillating events but as members of committed communities, rooted in the gospel and attentive to the needs of their particular places and times.

Chapter Nine

Liturgies of
Christian Belonging

AS I SUGGESTED EARLIER, there are two broad sets of practices that can foster healthier forms of belonging: practices of joining with our embodied communities and practices of redemptive participation in the public sphere. I'll recommend one practice in each category: going for a walk and subscribing aspirationally.

Walk

There are any number of practices that help us to root our identities outside the deformative spaces of the public sphere and belong more faithfully to our places: attend and serve a church, volunteer at community organizations, even hang out in the local McDonald's. But the simplest way to begin may be walking out your own front door. We live in a time when most trips through our neighborhoods begin by stepping into our cars, and even those trips can often be replaced by an order via Amazon or DoorDash. In this milieu, it can be a radical act to stroll through your neighborhood. More fundamentally, walking can be an antidote to the telescopic morality and disembodied communities forged through our screens. As Wendell Berry has it, "If you want to *see* where you are, you will have to get . . . out of your car, off your horse, and walk over the ground."[1] Many people discovered the joys of walking through their neighborhoods in the wake of the Covid-19 shutdowns; perhaps that disruption will serve to revive the art of walking.

Witnesses to the transformative power of this activity abound. Rebecca Solnit chronicles many of these in her book *Wanderlust: A History of Walking*.[2] As she notes, we tend to think of people who took famous solitary rambles through the countryside: Henry David Thoreau and his "saunters" through the Concord fields; John Muir's thousand-mile walk across the United States at the conclusion of the Civil War; Annie Dillard's explorations through pockets of suburban wildness; Wendell Berry's Sabbath walks through the woods. (Berry calls himself "a bad-weather churchgoer" because if the weather is good, he prefers walking to church attendance. For the record, I don't recommend skipping church to go for a walk, but these two activities are not mutually exclusive.)[3] Such walking tunes us to the seasons and rhythms of the natural world, but walking in urban or suburban contexts can be an equally vital and formative practice.

Gracy Olmstead lovingly recalls many walks she took with her grandfather through Moscow, Idaho. He had lived there for

---

[1] In this same essay, Berry points to Day as a model of this grounded approach: "When I think of the kind of worker the job requires, I think of Dorothy Day (if one can think of Dorothy Day herself, separate from the publicity that came as a result of her rarity), a person willing to go down and down into the daunting, humbling, almost hopeless local presence of the problem—to face the great problem one small life at a time." Wendell Berry, "Out of Your Car, Off Your Horse," in *Sex, Economy, Freedom & Community: Eight Essays* (New York: Pantheon, 1993), 20, 25.

[2] Rebecca Solnit, *Wanderlust: A History of Walking* (New York: Penguin, 2001).

[3] Henry David Thoreau, *Excursions*, ed. Joseph J. Moldenhauer, Writings of Henry D. Thoreau (Princeton, NJ: Princeton University Press, 2007), 185-223; John Muir, *A Thousand-Mile Walk to the Gulf* (Boston: Houghton Mifflin, 1916); Annie Dillard, *Pilgrim at Tinker Creek* (New York: HarperCollins, 2013); and Wendell Berry, *This Day: Collected & New Sabbath Poems, 1979–2012* (Berkeley, CA: Counterpoint, 2013), xxi.

decades, so "as we walked together, Grandpa would share stories about the homes we passed and their past or present inhabitants." Because this regular activity connected him to his place and his neighbors, she describes it as "a ritual of love": "Walking is a slow and porous experience. . . . To walk is also to be vulnerable: it forces us into physical interaction with surrounding streets, homes, and people. This can delay us, annoy us, even put us in danger. But it connects us to community in a way that cars never can." Olmstead admits that her walks near her new home in Alexandria, Virginia, have a different character from her long-rooted grandfather's walks: "I have not yet walked or loved a place as my grandfather did. I have not stayed put long enough. My walking is still more pilgrimage than it is loving liturgy."[4] Yet walking as pilgrimage can, over time, become walking as loving liturgy, a way of stitching one's life into the fabric of its place.

Chris Arnade provides a complementary account of the power of walking to shape and alter our belonging. Arnade was a successful Wall Street bond trader, but after the 2008 financial crash, he began to feel that his industry was deeply flawed; it had ruined the lives of many people, but those responsible for the destruction hadn't really suffered. He had long walked as a form of stress relief, but in 2011 he altered his routine, venturing into neighborhoods that his community considered dangerous:

> I first walked into the Hunts Point neighborhood of the Bronx because I had been told not to. I had been told it was too dangerous and too poor, and that I was too white. I had been told that "nobody goes there for anything but

[4]Gracy Olmstead, "The Art of the Stroll," *American Conservative*, August 14, 2018, www.theamericanconservative.com/articles/the-art-of-the-stroll/.

drugs and prostitutes." The people telling me this were my colleagues (other bankers), my neighbors (other wealthy Brooklynites), and my friends (other academics). All, like me, successful, well-educated people who had opinions on the Bronx but had never been there.[5]

As he walked through these neighborhoods, he talked with people, took portraits of them, and began to realize that their approach to life, though very different from his, made good sense. Arnade hadn't thought his "front-row" friends really *had* biases. Their views were objective, well informed, fact based. After all, he "read three papers daily" and watched documentaries and gave money to charity. But his walking—and what that walking led to, the hanging out in McDonald's, the slipping inside storefront churches, the conversations inside crack houses—proved to be a transformative act of joining, enabling him to think and feel from within a different community. By regularly walking in these neighborhoods, he caught the intuitions and affective responses of their residents. His new acquaintances had a very different approach to life than he and his coworkers did, but Arnade gradually came to understand their perspectives: "It didn't occur to us that what we valued . . . wasn't what everyone else wanted."[6] He went on to walk through many other American neighborhoods that most people with his background and education studiously avoid, and *Dignity*, the resulting book of interviews, stories, and photos, is a powerful testament to the lives and values of many "back-row" Americans.

These examples show how the simple practice of walking out your front door and down your street can reconfigure your

---

[5]Chris Arnade, *Dignity: Seeking Respect in Back Row America* (New York: Penguin, 2019), 1.
[6]Ibid., 3, 46.

relationship to your place and community. It is unfortunately true that, all too often, walking can be dangerous for women or minorities.[7] Garnette Cadogan writes movingly about the role walking played during his formative years in Kingston, Jamaica. When he moved to New Orleans and later New York City, however, he discovered that his dark skin made others fearful of him, and their fear put him in danger. The tragic reality is that "walking while black restricts the experience of walking, renders inaccessible the classic Romantic experience of walking alone." Despite these challenges, Cadogan continues walking because this practice is the only way he knows to make a place a home.[8]

As much as is safely possible, then, those of us who are tempted to find our communities and identities through the partisan, screen-mediated discourse of the public sphere would do well to take up the practice of walking. Walking can join us to our places and neighbors, rooting our sense of community and belonging in relationships formed outside the confines of the public sphere. Walking allows us to experience our places at a human pace and scale; it gets us outside of our two-ton capsules of metal and glass—and out from behind our six-ounce screens of metal and glass. As you walk, you might find yourself talking with a neighbor about a tree that fell down, or about who moved into the house that was for sale at the end of the street, or about the pestilential deer that keep eating their garden. The furor over the latest online outrage fades, and the reality and needs of your own place come into sharper focus.

---

[7]Solnit, *Wanderlust*, 232-46.
[8]Garnette Cadogan, "Walking While Black," *Literary Hub*, July 8, 2016, https:// lithub.com/walking-while-black/.

Subscribe Aspirationally

Unlike Frederick Douglass and Dorothy Day, most Christians will not found their own newspapers (though maybe you should!). But even if we don't launch news organizations that are committed to speaking on behalf of our communities, we can support such organizations by subscribing to their publications and being active participants in their work. If subscribing to a paper is a kind of formative liturgy, then we should be careful what publications we regularly read. Indeed, rather than diversifying our news feed or subscribing to papers across some artificial political spectrum, we should subscribe aspirationally: To what community do I want to belong? What newspaper or podcast or website gathers this community, articulating and shaping its values and perspective?

Because it is omnivorous and driven by a need to engage us, big news fractures our focus. We flit from scandal to scandal. But small publications—like Douglass's and Day's—can give sustained attention to particular issues and build a consensus around what is needed. So the return of partisan publications may actually be a good thing. From the commitment of *Civil Eats* to sustainable agriculture to the interest of *American Conservative* in a restrained foreign policy, new urbanism, and flourishing places, topically focused organizations can foster sustained, important discussions around challenging issues. Similarly, local newspapers and community newsletters focus on news that matters to a particular place, and they can play a vital role in fostering a community's consciousness. Even in the digital age, local news remains valuable and in many places continues to thrive.

In particular, look for—and patronize—writers and institutions who attend to the news from a longer, deeper perspective. Don't give your money or attention to websites that promulgate clickbait. Don't get your news from the TV; its financial incentives are such that it's almost impossible for a TV station to be anything but a frenetic peek-a-boo show.[9] This is a crucial consideration because the news shapes us not just through the arguments made by opinion columnists or talking heads; we are most deeply formed by the often unstated assumptions and biases that guide which stories are covered and how these stories are framed. When you watch or listen to or read the news, you are catching a community's ways of thinking—and feeling—about the events of the day. So seek out organizations that operate on a longer wavelength—not the moment-by-moment chatter of Twitter but the slower forms of thinking found in monthly or quarterly periodicals or in books. Even some websites work against the internet's presentist, secular bias by publishing book reviews and long-form essays.

Indeed, for all of its downsides, the internet offers opportunities for increased reader engagement, and many organizations work to use digital technologies to foster community. Granted, much online space is taken up by wannabe thought leaders and public intellectuals building up their individual platforms one hot take at a time. Along the margins, however, there are institutions dedicated to gathering people together to read about and respond to current events and ideas. Many of these don't look like traditional media organizations, but they do vital work: *The Rabbit Room* and *Christ and Pop Culture* host vibrant discussions in private Facebook groups. *Mockingbird* and the *Front Porch Republic* put on annual conferences where readers and writers can mingle and converse. *Mars Hill Audio Journal*, *Mere Orthodoxy*, and *The Witness* publish audio interviews or podcasts where hosts and guests

---

[9]Neil Postman, *Amusing Ourselves to Death: Public Discourse in the Age of Show Business* (New York: Penguin, 1986), 77.

model respectful, genuine dialogue. Amid the milling swarms of secular, mass society, such websites and journals shelter and sustain pockets of pilgrims, encouraging them on their journey toward the New Jerusalem.

How does all this play out in my own life? If I'm honest, I probably spend too much time following the news; I tend to write the books I need to read. I often listen to NPR while doing the dinner dishes. I have an online subscription to the *Washington Post*, and I read essays published by many different websites, from *Civil Eats* to *The Atlantic*, *The American Conservative* to *Mere Orthodoxy*, *Dissent* to *Hedgehog Review*, *Christianity Today* to the *New York Times*, *Commonweal* to *First Things*. I'm relatively active on Twitter, although not having a smartphone provides me a necessary distance from its frenetic atmosphere. All this allows me to follow the general discussions in the public sphere, but the news I read consistently and with greater attention comes from communities to which I aspire to belong: the *Jackson Citizen Patriot* (our town's local newspaper), *World Magazine*, *Plough Quarterly*, and, most recently, *Local Culture*.

Local Culture is the relatively new print journal published by the *Front Porch Republic*, which is a website I help edit. When I stumbled across *FPR* as a grad student, it was a beacon of hope. I was steadily reading through everything Wendell Berry had written, but I hadn't yet found a community that was reckoning with Berry's contrarian sanity. The conversations on *FPR*'s website and the people I met—and then became friends with—at the annual conferences proved to be the community I was looking for. These people were addressing, in their writing and their lives, the problems that Berry and others had helped me identify as some of the root challenges of our day: a dualism between body and soul, geographic and cultural deracination, addiction to growth, the replacement of virtues with technologies, and the blithe denial of all limits. Out of gratitude for this community, then, I agreed to serve as editor-in-chief of the website. Editing is time consuming and doesn't count for much in my academic career, but it provides invaluable opportunities to shape a public conversation about our day's pressing issues.[10]

Again, most readers aren't going to edit a website or publish essays or news stories, but we can all seek out healthy communities with whom to read the news. And these communities don't have to be mediated through the internet: start or join a book group where you can discuss important books over cups of tea. Give a friend a copy of a journal you subscribe to and talk about an article that challenged you. The point here is to avoid consuming the news as an isolated spectator. Such a habit is not only counterproductive; it can be downright toxic.

On Pilgrimage Together

By now I hope I've convinced you that reading the news isn't a good in and of itself, but also that it can be an instrumental good to journeying well with our Christian and non-Christian neighbors. Indeed, *journey* is etymologically related to *journal*: both derive from a Latin word meaning "of or belonging to a day." At its best, the news provides the information and community we need to journey well on our path toward God. Dorothy Day seems to have had this etymology in mind when she titled her column in the *Catholic Worker* first "Day by Day" and later, perhaps regretting the pun, changed it to "On

---

[10]Parts of this paragraph are adapted from the post I wrote when I took up the editorial reins at *Front Porch Republic*. Jeffrey Bilbro, "Reviving the Conversation on the Porch," *Front Porch Republic*, February 8, 2018, www.frontporch republic.com/2018/02/reviving-the-fpr-conversation/.

Pilgrimage."[11] My friend Eric Miller makes even more explicit the transcendent goods that the news can serve. In a conference paper reflecting on the journal *Temenos* and the community it sustained among those who, for all their disagreements with one another, were united by their rejection of modernity's reductive materialism, he concludes,

> That a crisis of such historic proportions should be met with a journal is curious. A journal is an exceedingly modest affair, after all, born of the hope that human beings, trailing one another from page to page, might just be listening, and listening keenly, to one another. Journals are quiet. But . . . if the renewal of civilization—or the academy, or even a single soul—certainly requires more than a journal, it's hard to imagine the success of such a journey without it. Journaling together, day by day, we may just find ourselves nearer to that sacred place for which our fractured souls so palpably yearn.[12]

Reading the news will not save a single soul, but journals and the vibrant communities of wayfarers they gather can be indispensable guides as we seek to faithfully enact God's divine drama of redemption in our particular place and time. May we "fare forward" together as we strive

> to apprehend
> The point of intersection of the timeless
> With time.[13]

---

[11]Nancy L. Roberts, "Dorothy Day: Editor and Advocacy Journalist," in *Revolution of the Heart: Essays on the Catholic Worker*, ed. Patrick Coy (Philadelphia: Temple University Press, 1988), 123.

[12]Eric Miller, "'That Unageing Spiritual Reality': Kathleen Raine, *Temenos*, and the Hope of Civilization," paper presented at History and the Search for Meaning: The Conference on Faith and History at 50, Calvin College, 2018.

[13]T. S. Eliot, "The Dry Salvages," *Collected Poems, 1909–1962* (New York: Harcourt Brace Jovanovich, 1991), 198.

Bibliography

Allen, Danielle, and Justin Pottle. *Democratic Knowledge and the Problem of Faction.* Knight Foundation, 2018. https://kf-site-production.s3.amazonaws.com/media_elements/files/000/000/152/original/Topos_KF_White-Paper_Allen_V2.pdf.

Anderson, Benedict R. O'G. *Imagined Communities: Reflections on the Origin and Spread of Nationalism.* Rev. ed. London: Verso, 2006.

Arnade, Chris. *Dignity: Seeking Respect in Back Row America.* New York: Penguin, 2019.

Auden, W. H. *Collected Poems.* Reprint edition. New York: Vintage, 1991.

Auerbach, Erich. *Literary Language and Its Public in Late Latin Antiquity and in the Middle Ages.* Translated by Ralph Manheim. New York: Pantheon, 1965.

———. *Mimesis: The Representation of Reality in Western Literature.* Translated by Willard R. Trask. 50th anniv. ed. Princeton, NJ: Princeton University Press, 2013.

———. "On the Political Theory of Pascal." In *Scenes from the Drama of European Literature*, 101-29. Theory and History of Literature 9. Minneapolis: University of Minnesota Press, 1984.

———. *Scenes from the Drama of European Literature.* Theory and History of Literature 9. Minneapolis: University of Minnesota Press, 1984.

Augustine. *On Christian Teaching.* Translated by R. P. H. Green. Oxford: Oxford University Press, 2008.

———. *The City of God, Books VIII–XVI.* Translated by Gerald G. Walsh and Grace Monahan. Fathers of the Church: A New Translation 14. Washington, DC: Catholic University of America Press, 2010.

Baker, Jack R., and Jeffrey Bilbro. *Wendell Berry and Higher Education: Cultivating Virtues of Place.* Culture of the Land. Lexington: University Press of Kentucky, 2017.

Baker, Jack R., Jeffrey Bilbro, and Daniel Train, eds. *The Saint John's Bible and Its Tradition: Illuminating Beauty in the Twenty-First Century.* Eugene, OR: Wipf & Stock, 2018.

Baskin, Jon. "Tired of Winning: D.C. Think Tanks, NYC Magazines and the Search for Public Intellect." *Point*, April 23, 2018. https://thepointmag.com/2018/politics/tired-of-winning.

Baudrillard, Jean. *Simulacra and Simulation.* Translated by Sheila Faria Glaser. Ann Arbor: University of Michigan Press, 1994.

Bauman, Zygmunt. *Does Ethics Have a Chance in a World of Consumers?* Institute for Human Sciences Vienna Lecture Series. Cambridge, MA: Harvard University Press, 2008.

Beer, Jeremy. *The Philanthropic Revolution: An Alternative History of American Charity.* Philadelphia: University of Pennsylvania Press, 2015.

Berry, Wendell. "In Defense of Literacy." In *A Continuous Harmony: Essays Cultural and Agricultural*, 169-73. San Diego: Harcourt Brace, 1972.

———. *New Collected Poems.* Berkeley, CA: Counterpoint, 2012.

———. "Out of Your Car, Off Your Horse." In *Sex, Economy, Freedom & Community: Eight Essays*, 19-26. New York: Pantheon, 1993.

———. "Pray Without Ceasing." In *That Distant Land: The Collected Stories*, 38-76. Washington, DC: Shoemaker & Hoard, 2004.

———. *This Day: Collected & New Sabbath Poems, 1979–2013.* Berkeley, CA: Counterpoint, 2013.

Bilbro, Jeffrey. "Fierce Velleity: Poetry as Antidote to Acedia." *Front Porch Republic*, February 20, 2019. www.frontporchrepublic.com/2019/02/fierce-velleity/.

———. "From Violence to Silence: The Rhetorical Means and Ends of Thomas Merton's Antipoetry." *Merton Annual: Studies in Culture, Spirituality and Social Concerns* 22 (2009): 120-49.

———. "Reviving the Conversation on the Porch." *Front Porch Republic*, February 8, 2018. www.frontporchrepublic.com/2018/02/reviving-the-fpr-conversation/.

———. "Thomas Merton's Contemplative Politics." *Front Porch Republic*, December 10, 2018. www.frontporchrepublic.com/2018/12/thomas-mertons-contemplative-politics/.

———. *Virtues of Renewal: Wendell Berry's Sustainable Forms*. Lexington: University Press of Kentucky, 2019.

Blackburn, Bonnie J., and Leofranc Holford-Strevens. *The Oxford Companion to the Year: An Exploration of Calendar Customs and Time-Reckoning*. Oxford: Oxford University Press, 1999.

Blight, David W. *Frederick Douglass: Prophet of Freedom*. New York: Simon & Schuster, 2020.

Boese, Alex. *The Museum of Hoaxes: A History of Outrageous Pranks and Deceptions*. New York: Plume, 2003.

Boorstin, Daniel J. *The Image: A Guide to Pseudo-Events in America*. New York: Vintage, 1992.

Borgmann, Albert. *Technology and the Character of Contemporary Life: A Philosophical Inquiry*. Chicago: University of Chicago Press, 1987.

Bremmer, Jan N. "Erich Auerbach and His Mimesis." *Poetics Today* 20, no. 1 (1999): 3-10.

Brooks, Jonathan. *Church Forsaken: Practicing Presence in Neglected Neighborhoods*. With a foreword by Sho Baraka. Downers Grove, IL: InterVarsity Press, 2018.

Brown, George Mackay. *Magnus*. London: Hogarth, 1973.

Bruegel, Pieter the Elder (c. 1525–1569). *Massacre of the Innocents*. Accessed July 22, 2020. www.rct.uk/collection/405787/massacre-of-the-innocents.

Burke, Edmund. *Reflections on the Revolution in France*. London: Penguin UK, 1982.

Burkeman, Oliver. "How the News Took Over Reality." *Guardian*, May 3, 2019. www.theguardian.com/news/2019/may/03/how-the-news-took-over-reality.

Cadogan, Garnette. "Walking While Black." *Literary Hub*, July 8, 2016. https://lithub.com/walking-while-black/.

Carney, Timothy P. *Alienated America: Why Some Places Thrive While Others Collapse*. New York: HarperCollins, 2019.

Carr, Nicholas. *The Shallows: What the Internet Is Doing to Our Brains*. New York: Norton, 2011.

Casper, Scott E., Jeffrey D. Groves, Stephen W. Nissenbaum, and Michael Winship, eds. *The Industrial Book, 1840–1880*. Vol. 3 of *A History of the Book in America*. Chapel Hill: University of North Carolina Press, 2007.

Cavanaugh, William T. *Being Consumed: Economics and Christian Desire*. Grand Rapids, MI: Eerdmans, 2008.

Certeau, Michel de. *The Practice of Everyday Life*. Translated by Steven Rendall. Berkeley: University of California Press, 2011.

Chesterton, G. K. *The Collected Works of G. K. Chesterton*. Vol. 7, *The Ball and the Cross, Manalive, The Flying Inn*. With introduction and notes by Iain T. Benson. San Francisco: Ignatius Press, 2004.

Chilton, Bruce. *Redeeming Time: The Wisdom of Ancient Jewish and Christian Festal Calendars*. Peabody, MA: Hendrickson, 2002.

Coates, Ta-Nehisi. *Between the World and Me*. New York: Random House, 2015.

Crawford, Matthew B. *The World Beyond Your Head: On Becoming an Individual in an Age of Distraction*. New York: Farrar, Straus & Giroux, 2015.

Crouch, Andy. *The Tech-Wise Family: Everyday Steps for Putting Technology in Its Proper Place*. Grand Rapids, MI: Baker Books, 2017.

Daniélou, Jean. *The Bible and the Liturgy*. Liturgical Studies 3. Notre Dame, IN: University of Notre Dame Press, 1956.

Dante Alighieri. *Aids to the Study of Dante*. Edited by Charles Allen Dinsmore. Boston: Houghton, Mifflin, 1903.

———. *The Divine Comedy*. Translated by Allen Mandelbaum. New York: Knopf, 1995.

Day, Dorothy. *The Long Loneliness: The Autobiography of the Legendary Catholic Social Activist*. San Francisco: HarperCollins, 1997.

Declercq, Georges. *Anno Domini: The Origins of the Christian Era*. Turnhout, Belgium: Brepols, 2000.

DeMeré, Nichole Elizabeth. "How to Diversify Your Twitter Feed—and Why You Should." *Social Media Today*, July 25, 2018. www.socialmediatoday.com/news/how-to-diversify-your-twitter-feed-and-why-you-should/528438/.

Deneen, Patrick J. *Why Liberalism Failed*. New Haven, CT: Yale University Press, 2018.

Dickens, Charles. *Bleak House*. Oxford: Oxford University Press, 1998.

Dilbeck, D. H. *Frederick Douglass: America's Prophet*. Chapel Hill: University of North Carolina Press, 2018.

Dillard, Annie. *Pilgrim at Tinker Creek*. New York: HarperCollins, 2013.

Dix, Gregory. *The Shape of the Liturgy*. London: Continuum, 2005.

Doctorow, Cory. "Writing in the Age of Distraction." *Locus Magazine*, January 2009. www.locusmag.com/Features/2009/01/cory-doctorow-writing-in-age-of.html.

Donougho, Martin. "Hegel as Philosopher of the Temporal [*Irdischen*] World: On the Dialectics of Narrative." In *Hegel and the Tradition: Essays in Honour of H. S. Harris*, edited by Michael Baur and John Russon, 111-39. Toronto: University of Toronto Press, 1997.

Douglass, Frederick. "Our Paper and Its Prospects." *North Star*, December 3, 1847.

———. "To Our Oppressed Countrymen." *North Star*, December 3, 1847.

Douglass, Frederick, and Harriet Jacobs. *Narrative of the Life of Frederick Douglass, an American Slave & Incidents in the Life of a Slave Girl*. With an introduction by Kwame Anthony Appiah. New York: Random House, 2004.

Douthat, Ross. "The Covington Scissor." *New York Times*, January 22, 2019, Opinion. www.nytimes.com/2019/01/22/opinion/covington-catholic-march-for-life.html.

———. "The Stories That Divide Us." *New York Times*, July 27, 2019, Opinion. www.nytimes.com/2019/07/27/opinion/sunday/the-stories-that-divide-us.html.

Dudek, Louis. *Literature and the Press: A History of Printing, Printed Media, and Their Relation to Literature*. Toronto: Ryerson Press, 1960.

Earley, Justin Whitmel. *The Common Rule: Habits of Purpose for an Age of Distraction*. Downers Grove, IL: InterVarsity Press, 2019.

Eisenstein, Elizabeth L. *The Printing Press as an Agent of Change: Communications and Cultural Transformations in Early Modern Europe*. Cambridge: Cambridge University Press, 1980.

Eliot, T. S. *Collected Poems, 1909–1962*. New York: Harcourt Brace Jovanovich, 1991.

Ellul, Jacques. *Propaganda: The Formation of Men's Attitudes*. New York: Vintage, 1973.

Farhi, Paul. "The Washington Post's New Slogan Turns Out to Be an Old Saying." *Washington Post*, February 24, 2017, Style. www.washingtonpost.com/lifestyle/style/the

-washington-posts-new-slogan-turns-out-to-be-an-old-saying/2017/02/23/cb19
9cda-fa02-11e6-be05-1a3817ac21a5_story.html.

Flanagan, Caitlin. "The Media Botched the Covington Catholic Story." *Atlantic*, January
23, 2019. www.theatlantic.com/ideas/archive/2019/01/media-must-learn-covington
-catholic-story/581035/.

Friedman, Mira. "Marc Chagall's Portrayal of the Prophet Jeremiah." *Zeitschrift für
Kunstgeschichte* 47, no. 3 (1984): 374-91.

Fukuyama, Francis. "The End of History?" *National Interest*, no. 16 (1989): 3-18.

———. *The End of History and the Last Man*. New York: Simon & Schuster, 2006.

Funke, Daniel. "Snopes Has Its Site Back: But the Legal Battle over Its Ownership Will
Drag on for Months." Poynter Institute, March 20, 2018. www.poynter.org/fact
-checking/2018/snopes-has-its-site-back-but-the-legal-battle-over-its-ownership
-will-drag-on-for-months/.

Gadamer, Hans-Georg. *Truth and Method*. Translated by Joel Weinsheimer and Donald
G. Marshall. Rev. ed. London: Sheed & Ward, 1999.

Governor, James. "Why I Started Following a More Diverse Set of People on Twitter."
RedMonk, April 12, 2018. https://redmonk.com/jgovernor/2018/04/12/why-i-started
-following-a-more-diverse-set-of-people-on-twitter/.

Graham, David A. "The Wrong Side of 'the Right Side of History.'" *Atlantic*, December 21,
2015. www.theatlantic.com/politics/archive/2015/12/obama-right-side-of-history
/420462/.

Grant, George Parkin. *Time as History*. Edited with an introduction by William Christian.
Toronto: University of Toronto Press, 1995.

Greenfield, Susan. *Mind Change: How Digital Technologies Are Leaving Their Mark
on Our Brains*. New York: Random House, 2015.

Griffiths, Paul J. *Decreation: The Last Things of All Creatures*. Waco, TX: Baylor University Press, 2014.

———. *Intellectual Appetite: A Theological Grammar*. Washington, DC: Catholic University of America Press, 2009.

Gross, Robert A., and Mary Kelley, eds. *An Extensive Republic: Print, Culture, and Society
in the New Nation, 1790–1840*. Vol. 2 of *A History of the Book in America*. Chapel Hill:
University of North Carolina Press, 2010.

Gurri, Adam. "Free Yourself from the Telescopic Morality Machine." *Front Porch Republic*, December 9, 2014. www.frontporchrepublic.com/2014/12/free-telescopic
-morality-machine/.

Haidt, Jonathan. *The Righteous Mind: Why Good People Are Divided by Politics and
Religion*. New York: Vintage, 2013.

Haidt, Jonathan, and Tobias Rose-Stockwell. "The Dark Psychology of Social Networks."
Atlantic, December 2019. www.theatlantic.com/magazine/archive/2019/12/social
-media-democracy/600763/.

Han, Byung-Chul. *In the Swarm: Digital Prospects*. Translated by Erik Butler. Cambridge, MA: MIT Press, 2017.

Havers, Grant. "A Christian Hegel in Canada." *Modern Age*, Winter 2019, 51-59.

Heath, Chip, and Dan Heath. *Switch: How to Change Things When Change Is Hard*.
New York: Crown, 2010.

Hegel, Georg Wilhelm Friedrich. *Miscellaneous Writings of G. W. F. Hegel*. Edited by Jon
Stewart. Evanston, IL: Northwestern University Press, 2002.

Hersh, Eitan. "College-Educated Voters Are Ruining American Politics." *Atlantic*, January 20, 2020. www.theatlantic.com/ideas/archive/2020/01/political-hobbyists -are-ruining-politics/605212/.

Hoe, Robert. *A Short History of the Printing Press and of the Improvements in Printing Machinery from the Time of Gutenberg up to the Present Day (1902)*. New York: Robert Hoe, 1902.

Illich, Ivan. *In the Vineyard of the Text: A Commentary to Hugh's "Didascalicon."* Chicago: University of Chicago Press, 1993.

———. *Tools for Conviviality*. London: Marion Boyars, 2001.

Jacobs, Alan. "After Technopoly." *New Atlantis* 58 (Spring 2019): 3-14.

———. *Breaking Bread with the Dead: A Reader's Guide to a More Tranquil Mind*. New York: Penguin, 2020.

———. "Habits of Mind in an Age of Distraction." *Comment*, June 1, 2016, 38-46.

———. *How to Think: A Survival Guide for a World at Odds*. New York: Currency, 2017.

———. *The Pleasures of Reading in an Age of Distraction*. New York: Oxford University Press, 2011.

Jean-Charles, Nault. *The Noonday Devil: Acedia, the Unnamed Evil of Our Times*. San Francisco: Ignatius Press, 2015.

Jeffrey, David Lyle. *The Early English Lyric and Franciscan Spirituality*. Lincoln: University of Nebraska Press, 1975.

———. "Franciscan Spirituality and the Rise of Early English Drama." *Mosaic: A Journal for the Interdisciplinary Study of Literature* 8, no. 4 (1975): 17-46.

———. *In the Beauty of Holiness: Art and the Bible in Western Culture*. Grand Rapids, MI: Eerdmans, 2017.

———. *People of the Book: Christian Identity and Literary Culture*. Grand Rapids, MI: Eerdmans, 1996.

Jennings, Willie James. *The Christian Imagination: Theology and the Origins of Race*. New Haven, CT: Yale University Press, 2010.

———. "My Anger, God's Righteous Indignation (Response to the Death of George Floyd)." *For the Life of the World*. Accessed July 21, 2020. https://for-the-life-of-the-world -yale-center-for-faith-culture.simplecast.com/episodes/my-anger-gods-righteous -indignation-willie-jennings-response-to-the-death-of-george-floyd-FXkkWh9b.

Jones, David. *The Anathemata*. London: Faber & Faber, 2010.

Joseph, Andrew. "'We Don't Actually Have That Answer Yet': WHO Clarifies Comments on Asymptomatic Spread of Covid-19." *STAT*, June 9, 2020. www.statnews.com /2020/06/09/who-comments-asymptomatic-spread-covid-19/.

Kahneman, Daniel. *Thinking, Fast and Slow*. New York: Farrar, Straus & Giroux, 2011.

Kessler, Glenn. "About the Fact Checker." *Washington Post*, January 1, 2017. www.wash ingtonpost.com/politics/2019/01/07/about-fact-checker/.

Kingsolver, Barbara. "The One-Eyed Monster, and Why I Don't Let Him In." In *Small Wonder: Essays*, 131-43. New York: Harper Perennial, 2003.

Klein, Ezra. "Why the Most Informed Voters Are Often the Most Badly Misled." *Vox*, June 8, 2015. www.vox.com/2015/6/8/8740897/informed-voters-may-not-be-better-voters.

Klein, Ezra, and Ta-Nehisi Coates. "Ta-Nehisi Coates: 'I'm a Big Believer in Chaos.'" *Vox*, December 19, 2016. www.vox.com/conversations/2016/12/19/13952578/ta-nehisi -coates-ezra-klein.

Kosmin, Paul J. *Time and Its Adversaries in the Seleucid Empire*. Cambridge, MA: Belknap Press of Harvard University Press, 2018.

Langlands, Alexander. *Cræft: An Inquiry into the Origins and True Meaning of Traditional Crafts*. New York: Norton, 2019.

Lasch, Christopher. *The Revolt of the Elites and the Betrayal of Democracy*. New York: Norton, 1995.

———. *The True and Only Heaven: Progress and Its Critics*. New York: Norton, 1991.

Latour, Bruno. *Down to Earth: Politics in the New Climatic Regime*. English edition. Cambridge: Polity Press, 2018.

Levin, Yuval. "Tribalism Comes for Pandemic Science." *New Atlantis*, June 5, 2020. www.thenewatlantis.com/publications/tribalism-comes-for-pandemic-science.

Lewis, C. S. *The Abolition of Man*. San Francisco: HarperOne, 2009.

———. *The Discarded Image: An Introduction to Medieval and Renaissance Literature*. Cambridge: Cambridge University Press, 2012.

———. *The Four Loves*. New York: Harcourt Brace, 1988.

———. "The Inner Ring." In *The Weight of Glory, and Other Addresses*, 55-66. New York: Macmillan, 1949.

———. *Mere Christianity*. San Francisco: HarperOne, 2015.

———. "On the Reading of Old Books." In *God in the Dock: Essays on Theology and Ethics*, 200-207. Grand Rapids, MI: Eerdmans, 1970.

Lyotard, Jean-François. *The Postmodern Condition: A Report on Knowledge*. Translated by Geoff Bennington and Brian Massumi. Minneapolis: University of Minnesota Press, 1984.

MacIntyre, Alasdair. *Whose Justice? Which Rationality?* Notre Dame, IN: University of Notre Dame Press, 1989.

Madrigal, Alexis C. "What Facebook Did to American Democracy." *The Atlantic*, October 12, 2017. https://www.theatlantic.com/technology/archive/2017/10/what-facebook-did/542502/.

McEntyre, Marilyn. *Caring for Words in a Culture of Lies*. Grand Rapids, MI: Eerdmans, 2009.

McKelvey, Douglas Kaine. *Every Moment Holy*. Nashville: Rabbit Room Press, 2017.

Merton, Thomas. *The Asian Journal of Thomas Merton*. Rev. ed. Edited by Patrick Hart, James Laughlin, Naomi Burton Stone, and Amiya Chakravarty. New York: New Directions, 1975.

———. *The Collected Poems of Thomas Merton*. New York: New Directions, 1980.

———. *My Argument with the Gestapo*. New York: New Directions, 1975.

———. *The Secular Journal of Thomas Merton*. New York: Farrar, Straus & Cudahy, 1959.

———. *Seeds of Destruction*. New York: Farrar, Straus & Giroux, 1965.

———. *The Sign of Jonas*. New York: Harvest Books, 1981.

———. *Thomas Merton on Peace*. New York: McCall, 1971.

Mikkelson, David. "Why We Include Humor and Satire in Snopes.Com." Snopes.com, August 15, 2019. www.snopes.com/notes/why-we-include-humor-and-satire-in-snopes-com/.

Miller, Eric. "'That Unageing Spiritual Reality': Kathleen Raine, *Temenos* and the Hope of Civilization." Paper presented at History and the Search for Meaning: The Conference on Faith and History at 50, Calvin College, October 5, 2018.

Mitchell, J. B. "Address of Welcome." *Publishers Weekly* 10 (1876): 167.

Mounk, Yascha. "Republicans Don't Understand Democrats—and Democrats Don't Understand Republicans." *Atlantic*, June 23, 2019. www.theatlantic.com/ideas/archive/2019/06/republicans-and-democrats-dont-understand-each-other/592324/.

Muir, John. *A Thousand-Mile Walk to the Gulf*. Boston: Houghton Mifflin, 1916.

Neheli, Nicole Blanchett. "Here's How Metrics and Analytics Are Changing Newsroom Practice." *JSource*, February 20, 2019. https://j-source.ca/article/heres-how-metrics -and-analytics-are-changing-newsroom-practice/.

Nisbet, Robert. *The Quest for Community: A Study in the Ethics of Order and Freedom.* Wilmington, DE: Intercollegiate Studies Institute, 2010.

Norris, Kathleen. *The Quotidian Mysteries: Laundry, Liturgy and "Women's Work."* New York: Paulist Press, 1998.

Nouwen, Henri J. M. *Thomas Merton: Contemplative Critic.* San Francisco: Harper & Row, 1981.

Obama, Barack. "Barack Obama Victory Speech." *C-Span*, November 4, 2008. www.c-span .org/video/?282164-2/barack-obama-victory-speech.

———. "Inaugural Address by President Barack Obama." White House news release, January 21, 2013. https://obamawhitehouse.archives.gov/the-press-office/2013 /01/21/inaugural-address-president-barack-obama.

O'Connell, Patrick F. *Cables to the Ace, or Familiar Liturgies of Misunderstanding.* In *The Thomas Merton Encyclopedia*, edited by William H. Shannon, Christine M. Bochen, and Patrick F. O'Connell, 36-38. Maryknoll, NY: Orbis Books, 2002.

Olasky, Marvin. *Reforming Journalism.* Phillipsburg, NJ: P&R, 2019.

Olmstead, Gracy. "The Art of the Stroll." *American Conservative*, August 14, 2018. www .theamericanconservative.com/articles/the-art-of-the-stroll/.

Ong, Walter J. *Orality and Literacy: The Technologizing of the Word.* New Accents. London: Routledge, 1991.

———. *Ramus, Method, and the Decay of Dialogue: From the Art of Discourse to the Art of Reason.* Chicago: University of Chicago Press, 2004.

Pascal, Blaise. *Blaise Pascal: Thoughts, Letters, Minor Works.* Translated by W. F. Trotter, M. L. Booth, and O. W. Wight. Harvard Classics 48. New York: P. F. Collier & Son, 1910.

Pétrement, Simone. *Simone Weil: A Life.* New York: Pantheon Books, 1976.

Pieper, Josef. *Only the Lover Sings: Art and Contemplation.* Translated by Lothar Krauth. San Francisco: Ignatius Press, 1990.

Pinkard, Terry P. *Hegel: A Biography.* Cambridge: Cambridge University Press, 2000.

Pinker, Steven. *The Better Angels of Our Nature: Why Violence Has Declined.* New York: Penguin, 2012.

———. *Enlightenment Now: The Case for Reason, Science, Humanism, and Progress.* New York: Penguin, 2019.

Polanyi, Michael. *The Tacit Dimension.* 1966. Reprint, Chicago: University of Chicago Press, 2009.

Postman, Neil. *Amusing Ourselves to Death: Public Discourse in the Age of Show Business.* New York: Penguin, 1986.

Prime Minister's Office, UK. "PM Launches Government's First Loneliness Strategy." Press release, October 15, 2018. www.gov.uk/government/news/pm-launches -governments-first-loneliness-strategy.

Pulitzer Prizes. "Art Cullen of *The Storm Lake Times*, Storm Lake, IA," 2017. www.pulitzer .org/winners/art-cullen.

Putnam, Robert D. *Bowling Alone: The Collapse and Revival of American Community.* New York: Touchstone, 2001.

Radner, Ephraim. *Leviticus.* Grand Rapids, MI: Brazos Press, 2008.

Reinders, Philip F., author and compiler. *Seeking God's Face: Praying with the Bible Through the Year.* Grand Rapids, MI: Faith Alive Christian Resources, 2010.

Roberts, Nancy L. "Dorothy Day: Editor and Advocacy Journalist." In *Revolution of the Heart: Essays on the Catholic Worker*, edited by Patrick Coy, 115-33. Philadelphia: Temple University Press, 1988.

Robinson, Marilynne. *The Givenness of Things: Essays*. New York: Picador, 2015.

———. *Lila*. New York: Picador, 2014.

Rosenthal, Caitlin. *Accounting for Slavery: Masters and Management*. Cambridge, MA: Harvard University Press, 2018.

Said, Edward W. Introduction to *Mimesis: The Representation of Reality in Western Literature*, by Erich Auerbach, ix-xxxii. 50th anniv. ed. Princeton, NJ: Princeton University Press, 2013.

Schulz, Kathryn. "The Moral Judgments of Henry David Thoreau." *New Yorker*, October 12, 2015. www.newyorker.com/magazine/2015/10/19/pond-scum.

Shapiro, Ben. *The Right Side of History: How Reason and Moral Purpose Made the West Great*. New York: HarperCollins, 2019.

Smith, James K. A. *Desiring the Kingdom: Worship, Worldview, and Cultural Formation*. Cultural Liturgies 1. Grand Rapids, MI: Baker Academic, 2009.

———. *You Are What You Love: The Spiritual Power of Habit*. Grand Rapids, MI: Brazos Press, 2016.

Solnit, Rebecca. *Wanderlust: A History of Walking*. New York: Penguin, 2001.

Solomon, Robert C. *In the Spirit of Hegel*. Oxford: Oxford University Press, 1985.

Solzhenitsyn, Aleksandr Isaevich. *The Gulag Archipelago 1918–1956: An Experiment in Literary Investigation, Parts I-II*. Translated by Thomas P. Whitney. New York: Harper & Row, 1974.

Sommerville, C. John. *How the News Makes Us Dumb: The Death of Wisdom in an Information Society*. Downers Grove, IL: InterVarsity Press, 1999.

Spencer, David R. *The Yellow Journalism: The Press and America's Emergence as a World Power*. Evanston, IL: Northwestern University Press, 2007.

Stein, Stephen J. "A Notebook on the Apocalypse by Jonathan Edwards." *William and Mary Quarterly* 29, no. 4 (1972): 623–34.

Stewart, Katherine. "Why Trump Reigns as King Cyrus." *New York Times*, December 31, 2018, Opinion. www.nytimes.com/2018/12/31/opinion/trump-evangelicals-cyrus-king.html.

Stone, Linda. "Continuous Partial Attention." November 30, 2009. https://lindastone.net/2009/11/30/beyond-simple-multi-tasking-continuous-partial-attention/.

Strapagiel, Lauren. "This Woman Pretended to Be a Bush During Her Sister's Engagement and It's Pretty Funny." *BuzzFeed News*, September 30, 2019. www.buzzfeednews.com/article/laurenstrapagiel/sister-bush-proposal-ghillie-surprise.

Sunstein, Cass R. *#Republic: Divided Democracy in the Age of Social Media*. Princeton, NJ: Princeton University Press, 2017.

Talley, Thomas J. *The Origins of the Liturgical Year*. Emended ed. Collegeville, MN: Liturgical Press, 1991.

Taylor, Charles. *A Secular Age*. Cambridge, MA: Belknap Press of Harvard University Press, 2007.

Teilhard de Chardin, Pierre. *The Phenomenon of Man*. Translated by Bernard Wall. 1959. Reprint, New York: Harper Perennial Modern Thought, 2008.

Thaler, Richard H., and Cass R. Sunstein. *Nudge: Improving Decisions About Health, Wealth, and Happiness*. Rev. & exp. ed. New York: Penguin, 2009.

Thoreau, Henry David. *The Correspondence of Henry David Thoreau*. Edited by Walter Harding and Carl Bode. New York: New York University Press, 1958.

———. *Excursions*. Edited by Joseph J. Moldenhauer. Writings of Henry D. Thoreau. Princeton, NJ: Princeton University Press, 2007.

———. *Reform Papers*. Edited by Wendell Glick. Writings of Henry David Thoreau. Princeton, NJ: Princeton University Press, 1973.

———. *Walden and Civil Disobedience*. New York: Penguin Classics, 1983.

Tocqueville, Alexis de. *Democracy in America*. Translated by Arthur Goldhammer. New York: Library of America, 2004.

Tolkien, J. R. R. *The Fellowship of the Ring: Being the First Part of the Lord of the Rings*. New York: Ballantine, 2001.

Trump, Donald. "You Gonna Win So Much You May Even Get Tired of Winning." YouTube, May 20, 2016. www.youtube.com/watch?v=daOH-pTd_nk.

Tufekci, Zeynep. "How Social Media Took Us from Tahrir Square to Donald Trump." *MIT Technology Review*, August 14, 2018. www.technologyreview.com/s/611806/how-social-media-took-us-from-tahrir-square-to-donald-trump/.

———. *Twitter and Tear Gas: The Power and Fragility of Networked Protest*. New Haven, CT: Yale University Press, 2017.

Turkle, Sherry. *Alone Together: Why We Expect More from Technology and Less from Each Other*. New York: Basic Books, 2012.

Twenge, Jean M. *IGen: Why Today's Super-Connected Kids Are Growing Up Less Rebellious, More Tolerant, Less Happy—and Completely Unprepared for Adulthood—and What That Means for the Rest of Us*. New York: Simon & Schuster, 2017.

Vaidhyanathan, Siva. *Antisocial Media: How Facebook Disconnects Us and Undermines Democracy*. New York: Oxford University Press, 2018.

Walls, Laura Dassow. *Henry David Thoreau: A Life*. Chicago: University of Chicago Press, 2017.

Warren, Tish Harrison. *Liturgy of the Ordinary: Sacred Practices in Everyday Life*. Downers Grove, IL: InterVarsity Press, 2016.

Weaver, Richard M. *Ideas Have Consequences*. Exp. ed. Chicago: University of Chicago Press, 2013.

Wehner, Peter. "The Moral Universe of Timothy Keller." *Atlantic*, December 5, 2019. www.theatlantic.com/ideas/archive/2019/12/timothy-kellers-moral-universe/603001/.

Weil, Simone. *Waiting for God*. Translated by Emma Craufurd. New York: Harper & Row, 1973.

Weinacht, Aaron. "Time and Place in Eugene Vodolazkin's Imagination." *Front Porch Republic*, May 20, 2019. www.frontporchrepublic.com/2019/05/time-and-place-in-eugene-vodolazkins-imagination/.

West, Cornel, and Christa Buschendorf. *Black Prophetic Fire*. Boston: Beacon Press, 2015.

Williams, Thomas Chatterton. "We Often Accuse the Right of Distorting Science: But the Left Changed the Coronavirus Narrative Overnight." *Guardian*, June 8, 2020, Opinion. www.theguardian.com/commentisfree/2020/jun/08/we-often-accuse-the-right-of-distorting-science-but-the-left-changed-the-coronavirus-narrative-overnight.

Wullschlager, Jackie. *Chagall: A Biography*. New York: Knopf, 2008.

Young, Kevin. *Bunk: The Rise of Hoaxes, Humbug, Plagiarists, Phonies, Post-Facts, and Fake News*. Minneapolis: Graywolf Press, 2017.

Zimmerman, Martha. *Celebrate the Feasts of the Old Testament in Your Own Home or Church*. Bloomington, MN: Bethany House, 1981.

General Index

algorithms, 139-40

Allen, Danielle, 129, 134-35, 138, 151-52

Anderson, Benedict, 81, 121-26, 129, 146

antipoetry, 48-50

arc of history, 69-70, 74, 82-85, 89-90, 106

Arnade, Chris, 167-68

Auerbach, Erich, 69-71, 73-75, 78-81, 83, 86, 91, 96-101, 104, 108, 112, 123

Augustine, Saint, 22, 31, 75, 88-89, 91, 98, 148, 162

Bauman, Zygmunt, 131

Berry, Wendell, 16, 26-27, 112-13, 128, 138, 149, 155, 165-66, 172

Brown, George Mackay, 113

calendar, 67, 71-73, 81, 110-11

Catholic Worker, 157, 163, 173-74

Chagall, Marc, 33-35, 43, 54

chronos, 67-69, 71, 74-96, 99-109, 112-13, 116, 120-21, 124, 131

civil rights, 44, 47, 52-53

clickbait, 11, 23, 57, 170-71

Coates, Ta-Nehisi, 85-86

contemplative politics, 35, 43-55

curiosity, 22-23, 25

Dante, 5, 70, 75, 86, 88, 91, 101-4, 108, 112

Day of the Lord, 93-95, 108

Day, Dorothy, 5, 146, 157-58, 162-64, 166, 170, 173-74

democracy, 1-3, 6, 90, 132-33

Deneen, Patrick, 128

Dickens, Charles, 28-29, 79, 99

digital media, 2-3, 7, 11, 13, 20, 57, 81, 120, 126, 131-32, 134, 140, 149, 156, 170-71

Douglass, Frederick, 146, 157-62, 164, 170

Edwards, Jonathan, 105-6

Eisenstein, Elizabeth, 122, 130

Ellul, Jacques, 130-31, 139, 144

fact checking, 1, 120, 132-38, 141, 150-51

figural realism, 69, 71, 75-76, 86, 88-92, 97-108, 111-16

Francis, Saint, 75, 98

French Revolution, 79-80, 83-84

Front Porch Republic, 171-73

Fukuyama, Francis, 78, 86-87

Gandhi, Mahatma, 41

Garrison, William Lloyd, 160-61

Griffiths, Paul, 22, 39-40, 67-68, 90, 152

habits. *See* practices

Haidt, Jonathan, 120, 140, 147-48, 151-52

Hegel, Georg Wilhelm Friedrich, 75-80, 83, 90, 123, 144

historical realism, 71, 75, 78-79, 86, 99

hope, 37, 54-55, 82, 86, 95, 107-8, 172, 174

Illich, Ivan, 2-3, 116

incarnation, 71, 73, 76, 88, 90-91, 96-99, 153

intuition, 146-51, 157, 168

Jacobs, Alan, 58-59, 141, 149, 152-53

Jeffrey, David Lyle, 34, 92-95, 98, 101

Jennings, Willie, 107, 129, 153

Jones, David, 113

kairos, 67-69, 71-75, 88-96, 99-100, 103-4, 108-116, 120, 124

Kingsolver, Barbara, 30-31

Lasch, Christopher, 76-78, 82, 135-36

Latour, Bruno, 150

Lewis, C. S., 36, 59, 112, 119, 148

loneliness, 127-30, 141, 144, 159, 163

macadamized mind, 12, 16-20, 25, 32, 35, 51, 55, 57, 131

martyrs, 42-43, 54, 110, 113

Merton, Thomas, 5, 36, 43-55, 59-60

Nazis, 33, 44, 49, 70, 113

news feed, 3-4, 20, 23-25, 42, 51, 56-57, 59, 64, 75, 81, 85, 104, 116, 119-21, 133, 138-41, 149, 154, 156, 170

Norris, Kathleen, 61-62

North Star, 160-62

Obama, Barack, 82-83, 85, 137

Olmstead, Gracy, 166-67

partisanship, 4, 106, 120, 132-40, 143, 150-52, 169-70

Pascal, Blaise, 5, 35-43, 46-47, 51, 55, 70

Pieper, Joseph, 11, 25-26, 61-62

Plough Quarterly, 157, 172

Postman, Neil, 3, 14, 30, 46, 171

practices, 6-7, 56, 150-53, 164
    learn a craft, 61-64
    meditate on art keyed to kairos, 112-16
    practice kairos time, 109-112
    read the eternities, 56-61
    subscribe aspirationally, 170-73
    walk, 165-69

printing press, 2-3, 12-13, 122, 131, 155-56

prophets, 5, 88, 91-96, 107-8, 114, 161

Scripture Index